# AN OTHER BREED of CURRITUCK DUCK HUNTERS

# Another Breed of Currituck Duck Hunters

## Fresh Tales from a Native Gunner

TRAVIS MORRIS

Charleston · London

Published by The History Press
Charleston, SC 29403
www.historypress.net

Copyright © 2012 by Travis Morris
All rights reserved

First published 2012

Manufactured in the United States

ISBN 978.1.60949.749.1

Library of Congress CIP data applied for.

*Notice*: The information in this book is true and complete to the best of our knowledge. It is offered without guarantee on the part of the author or The History Press. The author and The History Press disclaim all liability in connection with the use of this book.

All rights reserved. No part of this book may be reproduced or transmitted in any form whatsoever without prior written permission from the publisher except in the case of brief quotations embodied in critical articles and reviews.

# Contents

| | |
|---|---|
| Acknowledgements | 7 |
| Introduction | 11 |
| | |
| Mark Marshall | 23 |
| Louis Davis | 34 |
| Chandler Sawyer | 40 |
| Chet Morris's Stories | 45 |
| Frank Helms | 48 |
| Barry Walker | 59 |
| Aaron Mathews | 68 |
| Dennis Lee Newbern | 72 |
| James Guard | 85 |
| Blanton Saunders | 96 |
| Hunting with an Eighty-Two-Year-Old Woman | 117 |
| The Intracoastal Waterway Trip of the *Deb Nan* | 123 |
| The *Wild Goose* | 139 |
| The *Frances M* | 141 |
| | |
| About the Author | 143 |

# Acknowledgements

I dedicate this book to my two grandsons: Chester Walton Morris II, "Chet," and Chandler Reed Sawyer. Chandler is six years older than Chet. Both of those boys started hunting with me at Piney Island Club when each of them got to be seven years old. I still had a gas boat and float box when Chandler was little. When I carried some of the club members across the sound while hunting, I'd take Chandler with me and let him shoot the cripples from the gas boat. He'd stay with me all day long and never complain. He didn't get to see clouds of ducks like I used to because they weren't there.

When Chandler was young, two of the club members from Columbia, South Carolina, got Chandler's mama to give him a note to get out of school a little early sometimes and go hunting with them in the afternoon and call ducks for them. I'd go pick him up. I just learned they'd slip him a little pocket change, too.

By the time Chet came along, I had quit using the gas boat and float box. Chet and his friend, Alex Evans, did get to hunt in it one time and had a good hunt, but they like to hunt in a scissor rig where they can take four or five people hunting at the same time.

Chet and I have had some good hunts together at Piney Island. He is a good shot and I love to watch him shoot.

One time when Chet and I were hunting at Piney Point, Chet was killing his ducks and my gun was hanging up. Chet said, "Granddaddy, it's time to

# Acknowledgements

*Left*: Chet Morris (left) and Chandler Sawyer. *Author's collection.*

*Below*: Chandler picking his first duck at Piney Island Club. *Author's collection.*

*Below*: Chet after a morning duck hunt with me at Piney Island Club. *Author's collection.*

put that gun in a glass case and buy you a new one." I decided he was right. My gun was a model 11 Remington that Mr. Joseph P. Knapp had given to Mr. Frank Brumsey in the early 1920s. Daddy bought it from Mr. Frank around 1927 for $65.00.

In the early 1940s, Mr. Ray Adams, owner of the Whalehead Club, gave daddy a new Belgium Browning, and daddy gave me that old Remington. It was the only gun I had ever had of my very own. The 410 and 20 gauges I was using were loaned to me. The old Browning is now in a glass case on loan to the Wildlife Resource Center in Corolla. I gave the Remington to Chet, and I bought myself a new model 1187 Remington.

# Acknowledgements

I used to take the boys and their friends hunting. Now they take me. I'm still capable of taking myself, but I prefer to go with them because I enjoy their company. They are good shots and I love to watch them shoot.

## People Who Have Made This Book Possible

I want to thank the following people who shared their stories and pictures to go in this book so they may be preserved for generations to come:

Mark Marshall and his wife, Melodie
Louis Davis
Chandler Sawyer
Chet Morris
Frank Helms and his wife, Brenda
Barry Walker
Aaron Mathews
Dennis Lee Newbern and Kelly
James Guard; his wife, Elaine; their daughter, Amy Blankenship, and her husband, Andy Blankenship
Larry Williams, for use of the tapes of Blanton Saunders
Last but not least, my daughter, Rhonda Lee Morris. Without her help cleaning up my act and getting things in the order the publisher wants them, this book and five of my previous books would not have been possible.

As always, I want to give Susan Davis, who wrote *The Whalehead Club: Reflections of Currituck Heritage*, credit for getting me started writing books and helping me get the first one in the order the publisher wanted it. I never had any intention of writing a book until she saw some of the stories I had written and insisted I write a book. Since I wrote the first book, people have been after me to write another one, and I've been doing it to preserve a little of Currituck history for future generations.

# Introduction

Currituck has been noted for duck hunting since the 1800s. In past books, I have written about duck hunting in Currituck as it was done in yesteryear. Duck hunting is so different now that I decided I needed to write some stories by some of the younger guides in Currituck. First, though, I need to tell you a little about the old way so you can compare it.

Before the days of the fast and powerful outboards, the guides had what we called gas boats. These were inboard motorboats, usually between 22 and 32 feet long. Most had cabins. Some had spray hoods. They were powered by engines taken out of an old car and hooked up straight. By that, I mean they didn't have any transmission. This meant that when you hit the starter, she was off and running. When you turned the switch off, she drifted. There was no water-cooled manifold. The manifold would get cherry red but was good to warm your hands by. The engine was at most times cooled by what we called a "kicker," which is a galvanized pipe going down through the bottom of the boat in back of the propeller. It had an elbow on it facing the propeller so the propeller would force water into it. Inside the boat would be a rubber hose running from the pipe to the engine. In cold weather, when we got back home in the evening we'd pull the hose off the engine, blow the water out of it with our mouth and throw the hose over the stern. The next morning she'd be ready to go.

If you were going across the sound to a stuck or point blind, you would pull a skiff about sixteen feet long with your decoys. You'd anchor the

# Introduction

My gas boat *Rhonda* on Jones railway in Waterlily. *Author's collection.*

gas boat just outside where your decoys would be tied. In early years, you just had a shoving pole. In later years, you had a little outboard motor with maybe 4 or 6 horsepower. The guide would tie out the decoys, then get his men out of the gas boat and put them in the box in the blind. Then he would go back to the gas boat and take it far enough away so as not to blare (scare up) the ducks. He'd anchor the gas boat, then come back to the blind, put his skiff in the skiffway (or skiff hide) and wait on his men.

There were no impoundments then. The diving ducks set out in rafts in the sound. The puddle ducks would be in ponds in the club marshes or around the marsh. The gas boats putting along didn't scare the ducks to death. If they were right in your way, they'd get up and fly a little ways and put back down.

Most of my guiding was from a two man float box. This was invented by Mr. Pat O'Neal after the old battery or sink box was outlawed. It was made similar to the battery with wings on it to hold the seas down. Two men would sit in it. They would be sitting level with the water, and their feet would be below the water. Bushes would be around it, but it was still a small object compared to a bush blind.

I had a twenty-four-foot gas boat named *Rhonda* with a cabin and a shelter cabin with side curtains and a back curtain. I had a gas heater in the cabin. It was comfortable in the coldest weather.

# Introduction

I had just finished painting my float box for the last time (2004). It will probably never go overboard again. This shows the float box without the bushes. *Author's collection.*

I carried the float box on a twenty-three-foot skiff (which I still have). It took two good men to pull it aboard. I also carried two hundred wood ducks and ninety canvas geese. That skiff was full!

Most of the time, "Hambone" Ambrose Twiford, helped me take sportsmen. There were a lot of places we would tie the box out. One of our favorite places was the Gull Rock. This is a shoal in the shape of a horseshoe with the open part facing south right in the middle of Currituck Sound between Jones Dock at Waterlily and the Currituck Beach (Corolla) Lighthouse. The water at normal tide was about two and a half to three feet deep. If the wind was blowing, you could lay in the lee of this shoal in most any kind of weather. It was just a matter of who could get there first.

We didn't leave the dock until the crack of dawn because we had to see where the ducks were using. If we saw a bunch of ducks and ran them up and they came back to the same place, that's where we'd tie her regardless of how deep the water was or how hard or soft the bottom was. I had two sixteen-foot shoving poles. I always carried a coil of line. If the wind was blowing too hard for us to pole, we'd tie a line on the stern of the gas boat and let her back and tie out or take up with that. About three feet back from the stem post on the skiff, I had a chock on the washboards on each side with a cleat on one side. If you put the line in that chock, you could pole her right

# Introduction

Float box tied out. *Author's collection.*

up beside the gas boat. If it was pulling from the stem post, you couldn't pole it off to the side to save your life.

If I didn't have sportsmen to carry, there were five of us that called ourselves the Roving Hunters who'd go out together. The other four were Baxter Williams, Fred Newbern, Vernon Lee Creekmore and Gordon Sawyer. I had a big block V-8 Oldsmobile in *Rhonda* at the time, and she'd pull that twenty-three-foot skiff loaded with decoys and float box on top up or down the sound wherever the ducks were. We were shooting redheads and canvasback, and we usually got our limit because all but Baxter and I were excellent shots. I always ran the gas boat. I included Baxter because he was a real close friend, a fair shot and fun to be around. He would fall overboard at least once a year, and I'd have to give him part of my clothes.

We put the men in the box. They each had a life cushion to sit on. We'd go off in the gas boat and just idle around. We seldom cut it off. If the men killed a duck or wanted us, they would wave a cushion. We had no radios. Now remember, we were shooting mostly canvasback and redheads and some blackheads (bluebills).

# Introduction

Towing the twenty-three-foot skiff with float box and decoys. *Author's collection.*

Baxter Williams and Travis Morris were lifelong friends from the time they were boys until Baxter's death 2001. *Author's collection.*

When we were guiding, Hambone and I would take turns sleeping and running the boat. We could watch what was going on in the rig with binoculars. This was not legal, but we could almost always swim a bunch of geese to our men. This is not as simple as it sounds. You have to stay far enough away from them that you don't scare the geese up but get them kind of drifting away from you. You never turn the exhaust toward them; you always turn the bow toward them when you are turning around. If you see the gander stick his head up and look all around, you better ease off because they're getting ready to get up. If I do say so myself, Hambone and I were both pretty good at swimming geese.

# Introduction

In the early fifties, before I was taking sportsmen with my own rig, I worked for Mr. Earl and Charlie Snowden two winters. They had three float box rigs. Mr. Earl ran one. His gas boat was the first boat I can ever remember Mr. Pat O'Neal building. It first had an old engine out of an old car in it. Soon Dr. Fondi, who Mr. Earl took hunting a lot, bought him a new Chrysler Crown Marine engine for the boat. The deal was he just had to take Dr. Fondi hunting when he wanted to go. Back then, this was the only gas boat I knew of outside of the club boats in Currituck Sound that had a marine engine. Average people just didn't have the money to buy them. I never thought I'd be able to own one.

I can't remember who helped Mr. Earl. Mr. Clair Doxey and Pudding Rawls ran one. This was an old thirty-two-foot battery boat that used to belong to Bells Island Club. Mr. Wallace Davis and I ran the other one. It was the old Tom Brumsey battery boat, which was also thirty-two feet. The Snowdens had a little camp and long dock over at Bells Island where we left from. Aubrey Snowden now lives where the camp was.

They had a lot of people that came from Ohio that wanted to shoot geese. All we did when I was working for them was swim geese. We always tied in

Snowden dock at Bells Island in 1962. Louis Snowden is sitting on the left. Earl Snowden is on right. *Courtesy of John Snowden Jr.*

# Introduction

Travis Morris and Bill Riddick putting Bill Riddick's float box over north of Dew's Island in 1984. *Author's collection.*

the north end of the sound and always got geese. When we got their limit, which was two apiece, we could go home.

In the early sixties, another person I used to help guide a float box with was Bill Riddick. He had Mr. Charlie Wright's old rig and kept it at John Wright Jr.'s landing on Deep Creek in Jarvisburg. Bill Riddick worked for the Employment Security Commission and was head of the farm labor in this area. There wasn't much to do in the wintertime and he could get off.

I had my own float rig then, but he had some men who came from Elkin, North Carolina. If he didn't have anybody to help him, I'd pitch in. When I was helping him, we were hunting south of the Narrows.

I liked to hunt with him because he'd bring biscuits from home and Gates County ham. He had a little stove in the cabin of the boat. After we got the men in the box, he'd cook that Gates County ham and make gravy. It makes me hungry just writing about it.

If I had men, and Hambone was fishing and couldn't go with me, Mr. Riddick would go with me. We both loved to be in Currituck Sound. When I ran Monkey Island Club and was short on guides, he'd help me there.

I started to name the float boxes that I can remember in Currituck Sound but decided I better not because I'd be sure to leave somebody out and hurt somebody's feelings, and that's the last thing I want to do.

# Introduction

Jones's dock at Waterlily, looking north. Looking closely, you see net skiffs, skiffs with float boxes on them, gas boats and skiffs tied out to stakes. The gas boat at left is Woodrow Whitson's. The one on the right is Jimmy Hayman's. I included this picture because this is something you will never see again, with all the wood boats. *Author's collection.*

Let me say before I start talking about these young boys that you will never know how much I miss the sound of starting up an old gas boat on a cold morning. It didn't matter if it had a Model A Ford, six cylinder Chevrolet, six cylinder Ford, 440 Oldsmobile, Chrysler Marine 318 or 350 Chevrolet with marine conversion—I've had all those type engines in gas boats, they all had straight exhaust pipes with water going through them and they all sounded good when you put her bow to the east and headed across Currituck Sound with steam rising up from the exhaust and clouds of ducks getting up in front of you. The younger generation won't miss that like I do because they have never seen it and never will.

## The Younger Generation

I'm going to include stories by some of the guides who use float blinds today. This is what they call a scissor rig. It is not a new invention. My daddy had Buck Allen, who lived in a camp at Mill Landing in Maple, North Carolina, make one for me when I was sixteen years old. I never liked to use them and still don't. My old scissor rig is hanging in my son's warehouse now.

The scissor rig is usually made from juniper wood two inches thick and ten or twelve inches wide. It has holes that are about an inch and a half in diameter and about two feet apart. There is one of these boards down each side and a board across the front. The board across the front has an inch-deep board on top and on the bottom that extends about ten inches

# Introduction

Chet Morris's scissor float rig. You throw the anchor, open up the sides, push it off the bow, stick the bushes in the holes, then open it up, back out and tie out the decoys. You then go back into the float blind, pull the sides together, put the plug with the string tied to it in the hole to hold the sides together and you are ready for the ducks. You just hope they come. *Author's collection.*

longer on each end than the main board. This is so the side boards fit in between the two one-inch boards, and you put a bolt in it so it will swing open and you can drive the boat in the blind. This blind is floating in the water and anchored. The back is just like the front, except each side is fastened to the side piece instead of having a bolt in it and cut in two in the middle. It has a little line that is fastened to one side. The other end of the line is fastened to a peg. You open the blind up to get in it. When you are in, you pull it together and stick the peg in the hole that is bored for that purpose.

You transport it by picking the front up and putting it on the bow cap of the boat. Then you swing the sides up on the washboards.

Some guides also have a 2x4 on two-inch blocks bolted to the washboards. It's made just like the floating blind, but with smaller bushes to help hide the hunters.

These rigs are usually on 18- to 23-foot boats. They like to have two guides and three sportsmen. They are usually powered by 150- to 225-hp motors.

# Introduction

Scissor blind with boat and men in blind. *Courtesy of Chet Morris.*

They hunt all over Currituck Sound and North River, wherever they think a duck might be. These days, a duck can't sit down in Currituck Sound or North River without being run up. To get rest, he has to go in an impoundment or the middle of Albemarle Sound.

I will also include stories by guides who use the traditional bush and point blinds. This type of hunting is just like it has always been except some of the guides have much more elaborate blinds than guides used to have.

I'm not going to attempt to name all the men and boys who guide duck hunters, because I don't know all of them. One reason I don't know them is the generation gap. I'm going to tell you about the ones that I do know. The ones I'm going to tell you about are men who guide sportsmen for hire, not just ones who take their friends hunting. The Currituck County Game Commission issues one hundred float blind licenses, so you can see there are many float blinds that people just hunt for themselves with their friends.

The last two stories in this book have nothing to do with duck hunting or Currituck. Have you ever seen the yachts going through the Intracoastal Waterway going to Florida and wondered how it would be to make that trip? I'm going to take you on that trip. I always wanted to make that trip, but never thought I'd be able to make it. We never know what life holds in store for us. Thanks to my friends, I've made that trip seven times. I made it from

# Introduction

Coinjock, North Carolina to Fort Lauderdale Florida and back one time on my own boat, the *Frances M*. I'm going to tell you about my first trip, which was with the Ferrell Brothers and the last one on the *Frances M*. I've wanted to tell these in every book since I started writing books but could never make them fit in. This time I decided I was going to include them, fit or not.

# Mark Marshall

Mark is not a native of the area, but has become a true Currituck. He loves Currituck Sound and what he does. That's not all he loves here. He met and married a Currituck girl, Melodie Bunch.

Mark was raised in Springfield, Ohio and hunted in that area and also learned to be a taxidermist. His daddy came to Currituck duck hunting every year for three or four years. In 1984, one of his daddy's buddies dropped out of the trip and his daddy called him at the last minute to see if he wanted to go. "Sure," he said. They stayed at Mrs. Barrett's hunting lodge, which was located between Aydlett and Poplar Branch. They hunted with Wayne Davenport and had a great time and a really good shoot. Mark said he got to be friends with Wayne, who was about his age.

Wayne told Mark, "If you want to come down here and guide, Mrs. Barrett could fill every day for you."

"Long story short," Mark told me, "I was down here by that Fall and she did fill every day; I've been booked ever since. I try to work things around to keep people satisfied the best I can. Sometimes I just have to turn people down. It just seems like people are starved for the opportunity to get out on Currituck Sound hunting. Sometimes they have good luck and sometimes they don't, but they still want to come back."

I asked Mark where most of his sportsmen come from. He said that about half of them at first were northerners and that the rest were from North Carolina. They were people he had done taxidermy work for

# Fresh Tales from a Native Gunner

When Mark Marshall came from Springfield, Ohio, to Currituck, not only did he fall in love with the duck hunting in Currituck, he fell in love with and married a native Currituck girl, Melodie Bunch. *Author's collection.*

Dock at Barrett's Hunting Lodge. This is between Aydlett and Poplar Branch. Mark Marshall with twenty-two snow geese in 1999. *Courtesy of Mark Marshall.*

# ANOTHER BREED OF CURRITUCK DUCK HUNTERS

Mark Marshall and Hugh Carpenter, who bought the hunting lodge from Mrs. Barrett. *Courtesy Mark Marshall.*

John Williams from Pittsboro, North Carolina, hunting with Mark Marshall. *Courtesy of Mark Marshall.*

from Pennsylvania and Ohio who had never seen a pretty duck such as a canvasback, redhead or pintail.

Then Mrs. Barrett sold out to Hugh Carpenter. He ran the Lodge for a while, and Mark still kept his men there. Then it was sold to Bill Jernigan. He stopped using it as a lodge ten or fifteen years ago. Then Mark worked out a deal with Terry Miles to keep his men at Midway Marina in Coinjock. Terry has four motel rooms over the dock house, each with a coffee maker, refrigerator and other amenities. He also has a little two room cottage.

Mark keeps his boat at Poplar Branch Landing where he has a slip. It's a short run from there to his blind on Taylor's Creek. He has a spray hood on his boat. That feels mighty good to sportsmen sitting under it on cold, blustery days on the way to and from his blinds. His blinds are 6x12, and there's a roof over the seat. He usually takes three men. He stays out until the county take-up time at 4:20 p.m., or until they get their limit or decide they just want to come on in early.

All the local hunters around the Coinjock area or ones who are passing through Coinjock stop at Kevin's Store for breakfast. It is right across the road from J.I. Hayman & Son Hardware & Building Supply. Kevin opens up at 4:30 a.m. His warming case has been stocked with all kinds of breakfast

Mark Marshall coming up to blind with new dog, Jet. *Courtesy of Mark Marshall.*

# Another Breed of Currituck Duck Hunters

Rob Jones, Mark Marshall and Mike Johnson. Jones and Johnson are from Kinston, North Carolina. *Courtesy Mark Marshall.*

Kevin's Store. Kevin Spain is standing behind the counter. Dottie Jordan, who works there, is also behind the counter. Schoolgirls are standing in front of the case with all the good breakfast sandwiches, which are continually replaced from the kitchen. When all the hunters were in there at 5:00 a.m., I didn't think to take a picture—I was too busy getting breakfast myself! *Author's collection.*

sandwiches and biscuits from Cindy's Kitchen. Cindy is Kevin's wife. I can personally attest that it's good food. He also has plenty of coffee.

When Mark came to Currituck and started guiding, people found out that he was also a taxidermist. He said it was kinda slow at first, but then it kept picking up until it got to where he keeps busy the rest of the year after hunting season.

He joined all the state and national taxidermy associations and started competing and going to seminars and slowly gained a following of people. In his competition, he received a North American Champion that's now in the Wildlife Museum in Corolla. Mark said he won a lot of things. His goal was to get his bird certification, which he got early on. He won the state and national shows and tied for third place in the world show. That was the last world show he ever went to. He said it cost a lot of money, and at that time, they didn't give prize money like they do now. He quit going to the shows in the 1990s.

Mark says now he stays real busy in the off season just trying to get the ducks done that folks bring him in the season. He said he doesn't get them all done from one year to the next. He still has fifteen or twenty to do from last year, and he has taken in forty-five this year with more to come.

This swan is in the Wildlife Museum in Corolla. It won the National North American Championship. *Courtesy of Mark Marshall.*

## ANOTHER BREED OF CURRITUCK DUCK HUNTERS

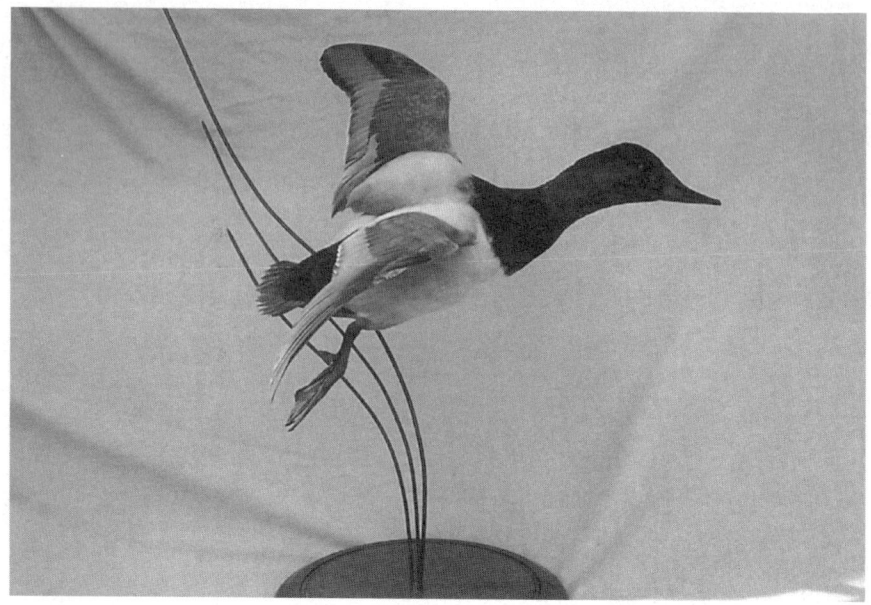

Flying canvasback. *Courtesy of Mark Marshall.*

Black duck. *Courtesy of Mark Marshall.*

# Fresh Tales from a Native Gunner

Pintails. *Courtesy of Mark Marshall.*

I later found out from Melodie that Mark also does some painting. She said a man named Stuart Ingram got up with Mark through Terry Miles (owner of Midway Marina in Coinjock). Stuart Ingram wanted Mark to do a waterfowl scene in a private museum of Coastal Carolina he had in Ocean Isle, North Carolina. He wanted Mark to do a diorama in a large room in the museum. Ingram told him to just do what he wanted to do as far as a Marsh scene with water, ducks, geese and swan. I wish I had room to show more pictures of this and wish you could see it in color because it is a beautiful diorama.

Mark said Mr. Ingram wanted a pair of every kind of duck that wintered in North Carolina. He had permits for Mark to collect them legally. He collected just about all of them and mounted them.

I asked Mark how he made that diorama. He said it has a large plywood floor. He first made the marsh scene, then painted the rest of the floor to look like water. He then poured resin over the whole thing and let that set up. Then he cut out holes in the plywood to put the swimming ducks in.

Mark said he did this work between 1993 and 1995. He said Stuart Ingram sold the museum to the Discovery Group from Charlotte, North Carolina. He doesn't know if they still own it or not.

# ANOTHER BREED OF CURRITUCK DUCK HUNTERS

Scenes from diorama Mark Marshall did for a museum at Ocean Isle Beach, North Carolina. *Courtesy of Mark Marshall.*

Scenes from diorama Mark Marshall did for museum at Ocean Isle Beach, North Carolina. *Courtesy of Mark Marshall.*

# Fresh Tales from a Native Gunner

Scenes from diorama Mark Marshall did for museum at Ocean Isle Beach, North Carolina. *Courtesy of Mark Marshall.*

Mark Marshall is a very talented person, as you can tell, but he keeps a very low profile.

The following are two stories in Mark's own words.

## Bad Day on the Sound

On January 14, 2005, Bit Twiddy and I took our old friends, Johnny Frys and Charles Lambert with two of their friends out hunting. We were in blinds less than a mile apart. The water was real high due to a persistent southwest wind, which was still blowing that morning. I knew a front was coming through that day, but wasn't sure when. I was hoping it would come late.

We were having a decent day and had a few ducks and a snow goose, when about mid-morning I noticed a black line of clouds moving down on us from the north. We hunkered in as a curtain of rain and wind hit.

It rained so hard you couldn't see the decoys, and the wind was ferocious, probably blowing 50 miles per hour.

When the rain slowed a little, I only had a handful of my 60–70 decoys in front of the blind. In a few more minutes I didn't have any. The water was piling up and it began to slap the bottom of the blind.

Usually after the headwind blows through, it settles down some, but not this day. It continued to howl through midday and into the afternoon. In a few minutes more, we were standing in knee-deep water in the blind. I looked at the boat and saw it heaving up (about even with my head) and crash back down, the motor inches from the walkway. Twice I went out and secured it better.

I had been in contact with Bit, and he was having a bad time too. We were waiting for it to slow down, so we could go in.

My wife called me and said a Deputy called wondering if I was hunting. The Coast Guard was at the landing and she went down there and spoke to them, and they recommended we not leave the blind. She asked if they were going back to get us. They said "no" as they pulled their boat out.

After talking it over, Bit and I decided to head to Tim Buck II in Corolla, which was maybe a mile ride for me. Melodie and Bit's son, Clayton, drove around to pick us up.

It was tricky getting loaded up and away from the blind, but we made the trip without incident. Anybody on the sound that day will not soon forget it.

## Good Day on the Sound

In 2002, during the split between the November season and the late season, we had a blast of cold air and days of hard north winds, which brought a lot of ducks down and pushed the water way out. I was hunting a blind on Thoroughfare Island. I had made a couple of trips out there in preparation for the Saturday opening day. On the shoals off the island, the game was really piled up: swan, geese and a ton of ducks, mostly Gadwall and Widgeon. I just hoped I could still get to the blind on Saturday.

Friday, the wind switched to the southwest and began blowing. It blew all afternoon and all night, and was still blowing on Saturday morning. The water came way up from what it was the day before, and those birds were looking for somewhere to go. They don't often come as hard and as fast as they did that day.

I had my buddies, Graham, Rob and Rom, with me that day, and they are a deadly crowd. We were done by 8:30 a.m. Mostly Gadwall and Widgeon. All agreed it was one of the best hunts we'd had in a long time.

Before leaving, I called my buddy, Bit Twiddy, who was in another blind with his brother, nephew and his nephew's son. I told him to get here fast because I was leaving. He hurried over there, and later, he told me they finished up about noon.

*You can contact Mark Marshall by writing him at 130 Bunch Road, Aydlett, NC, 27916, or call him at 252-453-3691.*

# Louis Davis

I have known Louis since he was a little boy. His daddy and mother bought Coinjock Marina in the late 1970s. I kept my boat there before I got a dock of my own. Louis was a cute little boy with an inquisitive mind. He could ask forty thousand questions. Maybe that's why he's done so well since he's been grown. He now owns Coinjock Marina and Restaurant. His step sister, Ginger, married my son, Walton Morris. They own Morris Farm Market in Barco, where all the antique tractors are. Their son (my grandson) Chet mates for Louis sometimes. Then sometimes Chet and my other grandson, Chandler Sawyer, take men for Louis in Chet's float rig or in Chandler's bush blind rig to Cedar Island Bay.

Louis started guiding for Watson Stuart in 1992, a couple of years after he got out of high school, and guided for him for eight years. This was back when Wayne Twiford Jr., Melvin Lewis and all those guys were guiding for Watson. Louis and a partner bought Coinjock Marina and Restaurant from Louis's daddy. Louis was hunting a lot after the boats had gone south for the winter, but just for fun. Going every day was expensive, plus it was hard to get a group together to go every day. That put him back to guiding. The money was good, and he got to bring some of his old clients back and he enjoyed it. He has since bought his partner out of the Marina and Restaurant.

I asked Louis where most of his clients come from. He said about half come from North Carolina, and everyone else from Illinois, Ohio, South Carolina, Georgia, Florida and all over. Some of his clients are people who

# Fresh Tales from a Native Gunner

Tray Mailaes, Larry Mailaes and Al Mailaes. Standing behind them is Louis Davis holding up the ducks. *Courtesy of Louis Davis.*

are going to Florida on yachts and find out about his guiding service while they are at the marina, then fly back up here during the hunting season. He gets most of his clients by word of mouth.

Three or four years ago, Louis guided a large group for Ducks Unlimited. They had a Southeast Conference, and he took the group duck hunting. These men were from all over the southeastern states. They had a good time with the combination of good hunting and good food. He got a lot of recommendations from that.

Louis is set up to guide about fifteen men per day. Breakfast is generally at Kevin's Store. If they are hunting close-by, he just tells the guides to meet in the Marina restaurant for lunch, or the restaurant will pack box lunches if they prefer. Some of the guides cook on the boat. Louis has a grill set up on his boat, and sometimes he cooks there. It just depends on where he is. Most of the time, they are going to get a hot lunch, and of course, a big meal for dinner. He said a lot of the hunters like it because they can go at their own pace. It's not six o'clock dinner. Whenever they are ready, they can wander over to the restaurant. Not being structured is kinda nice for a lot of them.

I asked Louis who guides for him besides Chet and Chandler. He named Donald Griggs, Jeremy Midgett, Thomas Newbern and several others who also guide part time for Watson Stuart, including Paul Garrett and Mike Labounty. Usually, though, it's just three or four of them. They can handle up to fifteen people and it's very seldom they need any more guides.

Louis uses both float blinds and bush blinds, but most of the guides prefer the float blinds. It depends on where the birds are. This year the concentration of birds was around Poplar Branch, and there is not a lot of room for float blinds to tie down there. You can't tie a float blind within five hundred yards of a licensed bush or point blind.

Louis said he'd had the most hunters he'd ever had this year (2011–2012), and it was one of the worst seasons we've had in a long time. The weather was warm, and the ducks just didn't come down here. He said his hunters were seasoned hunters and didn't complain. When it got really bad, he called every one of his parties a couple of days before they came and told them point blank that it was pitiful. The weather was warm and there didn't seem to be any weather on the horizon, and not many birds were around. He said nobody canceled. At one time he said he tried to cancel a few parties and they said, "You don't understand, Louis. At least you are seeing a few ducks. We've been going hunting at home all year and haven't seen a duck." They were hunting in swamps in the western part of the state and in South Carolina and places like that.

It's nice to see that some people still realize that duck hunting is not all about killing ducks; that's just a part of it. It's about being with friends who enjoy each other's company, being out on the water, appreciating seeing the sun come up over the horizon in the morning, cold wind on your face and seeing the glow of the sun falling behind the trees in the afternoon. Don't get me wrong. It's also nice to see a bunch of ducks set their wings to come in to the stools.

I've been duck hunting for seventy-one years. I've always found that true duck hunters, regardless of their walk in life, speak the same language. I've had many good friends over the years who wouldn't have given me the time of day if it hadn't been for the ducks. They travel in a different world from me, and we would have had no reason to have met. I just had a good example of that while typing this up.

# Fresh Tales from a Native Gunner

The phone rang, and it was John Bergwyn, who was my good friend Lindy Dunn's pilot for probably twenty years. Lindy has been dead since July 9, 2009. I devoted the last chapter in my book, *Untold Stories of Old Currituck Duck Clubs*, to Lindy. John and I were reminiscing about old times. He was talking about all Lindy's good friends that he'd flown over the years. Lindy owned The Guardian Corporation, which owned all the Hardee's restaurants in West Virginia, plus many other things. Lindy was one of my closest friends and I would never have met him had it not been for the ducks.

Currituck County has been lucky over the years, especially the early years, for the wealthy people who have come here and built hunting lodges and who have done things for the county, including giving people jobs. I've talked about that in some of my other books, so I won't get into it here.

Most of the guides today do it because they love it. If they didn't, they'd try to find another job because it's not easy work. They get paid well, but

Rick and Tom Simpson are brothers from Virginia. Rick is a member of the Churches Island Hunt Club, but they book at least one hunt for float blinding with Louis Davis every year. *Courtesy of Louis Davis.*

Clay Cartwright, George Munden and Doctor Jose Acostamadiedo. Note the bushes that go in the scissor rig. It looks like they had a good shoot of Teal. *Courtesy of Louis Davis.*

if you consider all the time and money it takes to rig all that equipment up, you'll find it's not cheap.

While I'm off the subject of Louis, I want to tell you about my other grandson who helps Louis some, Chandler Sawyer. He is a real good decoy carver. The problem is getting him to do it. He has been written up more than once in *Hunting & Fishing Collectibles* magazine. One time they had a three page spread on him. So much for my rambling. Now back to Louis.

Louis has a house next door to the restaurant that will sleep up to ten people, and the apartment over the restaurant sleeps five.

Louis started guiding in a seventeen-foot skiff before he got his dad's eighteen-foot Sea Hawk. Then he got an eighteen-foot Parker. This boat was a foot wider and made a big difference. He thought that was the only boat he'd ever need. Next, he got a twenty-one footer, and now he has a twenty-three-foot boat and is looking for one that's twenty-five feet.

He doesn't want to carry any more people, but everybody has so much gear now, and with three sportsmen, two guides and two dogs, that's a boat load.

# Fresh Tales from a Native Gunner

Now, let an old man tell you how this float blind hunting is today. I've been there and done that. I personally like more comfort than can be found in an open boat with a scissor rig. I've always had a cabin or spray hood on my boat whether it was a gas boat or skiff. With a scissor rig there is not room for a spray hood.

If you are hunting with somebody who hunts in a bush blind or point blind, they will most likely have a spray hood and the difference in comfort is like night and day. Sometimes you will kill more ducks in the float blind and sometimes more in the bush or point blind. The only thing I can say is the scissor rig float blind is the least comfortable.

*You can contact Louis Davis by writing him at 321 Waterlily Road, Coinjock, NC, 27923, or by calling him at Coinjock Marina at 252-453-3271, or on his cell phone at 252-202-1709.*

# Chandler Sawyer

The best duck hunting season my two grandsons have ever had was the 2010–2011 season. It was probably the best season we've had in Currituck in at least forty years.

One day when it snowed in 2010, Chet and Chandler were taking one party for Louis Davis. Donald Griggs and his mate, Jeremy Midgett, were taking another party for Louis, and Louis also had a party. All of them were using scissor float rigs. Louis tied off of Poplar Branch, while Chet and Chandler and Donald and Jeremy tied off of Dews Island.

Chandler said they'd tied out the rig and killed a duck or two, but weren't doing much. Louis came on the radio at about 10:00 a.m. and said he was done. He had his thirty ducks. They each had five men in the boat, and their limit was six ducks each. They had mostly Teal.

Louis said the ducks were still flying and whoever could get there first could climb in his rig, and he and his men would take their boat back to Poplar Branch Landing. As soon as he said that, Chet and Chandler told the men to unload their guns and get their stuff packed up. Chet and Chandler had already started snatching bushes out of the float blind.

As soon as they got the bushes out, Chet told the men to get in the back of the boat while he and Chet took up the decoys. Chet ran the boat, and Chandler picked up and stowed the seventy-five duck decoys and twenty-five goose decoys and got the float blind up on the boat. They were on their way to poplar Branch in eleven minutes!

When they got there, Louis and his men got in Chet's boat, and they got in Louis's rig. They soon got their thirty ducks—twenty-five Teal and five redheads. That was a day to remember. You don't get many days like that in a lifetime.

## CHANDLER'S BUSH BLIND

On this day, Chet and Chandler had a party for Louis, but they were in Chandler's boat. He has a twenty-one foot Carolina skiff with a spray hood and 150-horsepower Yamaha. They were leaving from Coinjock Marina and going to Chandler's blind, which is in the middle of Cedar Island Bay.

There were six men in the party. Louis and his mate had three of the men, and Chandler and Chet had three. The sportsmen had four Black Labs they had spent $18,000 on. Two of the dogs went with each rig, plus Chandler had his Chesapeake, "Chief."

Maybe I better stop here and tell you a little about Chandler's bush blind. First, you go into a "boat hide." You step up out of the boat and go through a little door into the box, which is four feet wide, twelve feet long and four

Chandler Sawyer's blind tied out in the middle of Cedar Island Bay. *Courtesy of Chandler Sawyer.*

# Another Breed of Currituck Duck Hunters

Chandler's dog Chief in the boat. *Courtesy of Chandler Sawyer.*

feet high, with bushes sticking up about another foot. There is a long bench to sit on and put your bag underneath. In front of you is a shelf to put shells, coffee, and other things on. Chandler has a bar stool in his end of the blind to kinda lean on and sometimes sit on. He's always on the lookout.

This blind was given to me sometime in the late forties by Mr. Norman Ballance, who was superintendent of Bells Island Club. The county game board passed a rule that the clubs couldn't have offshore blinds in their names. They could only have point blinds. At the time, I was too young to have the blind in my name and had to have it in daddy's name until I was old enough to have it in my name.

I'm getting old, and a few years ago, I got the blind put in Chandler's name because it's a good blind and I want him to have a place to hunt when I'm gone. Chet's daddy has my other blind that Mr. Norman gave me before he gave me this one, so Chet will have a blind.

Now back to the duck hunt. At the time, the blind didn't have a dog walk on it. This is a place built on the end of the blind where the dog can sit and see the ducks fall; there's a ramp going down to the water so the dog can get back in the blind. I never had a water dog. I was always the retriever. The boys have just gotten dogs in the last couple of years. Chandler and Chet's dogs have always stayed in the boat and gone out the back of the boat to get a duck. When he gets back with the duck, they pull him in the boat. They have since built a dog walk at that blind.

Everybody got up in the box, including the sportsmen's two dogs. Chief stayed in the boat the first day. The second day, Chandler left him home; there were just too many dogs. They were killing a few ducks. The dogs were all over everything, knocking things down and aggravating the crap out of everybody. Chandler was propped up against his stool, and all of a sudden, he felt this dog licking the back of his ear. Chandler turned around, and the dog had all four legs on the top of that bar stool like a circus elephant.

Some ducks came in, and they shot them. This dog was then sitting on the bar stool. He saw the ducks fall and sailed right out of the blind over the bushes and all. It's at least ten feet over the bushes and down to the water. He landed with a splash and went and got the duck. Chandler said they were good dogs, just high strung.

Chandler Sawyer's twenty-one foot Carolina skiff with spray hood folded down at Chandler's blind in Cedar Island Bay. Vicki Cronis, who provided this image, wrote a story for the Virginian pilot on Chandler duck hunting and a story on him carving decoys. *Courtesy of Vicki Cronis.*

# Another Breed of Currituck Duck Hunters

Chet and Chandler shooting from Chandler's blind. *Courtesy of Vicki Cronis.*

While all this was going on, Chet got a phone call from Louis saying he was so tired of picking dogs up out of the water he didn't know what to do. He said he told them that whoever owned those dogs was going to have to get down there and pick them up. They were hunting in a float blind.

I might add that when they have sportsmen hunting in Chandler's blind, they usually run back to the marina for a hot lunch. It's only about three miles and doesn't take long with a 150-horsepower motor on a twenty-one-foot Carolina skiff. It has a spray hood for the men to get under, so it's not a bad ride.

Chandler said the group they were guiding was from around the Raleigh area. He said most of the people they have guided are from the Raleigh, the Charlotte area or western North Carolina. Some are from South Carolina, and they had one man from Minneapolis, Minnesota.

All the people they carried were repeats from last year, and some of the same people came two or three times. I always found that you meet some nice people guiding sportsmen. Once in a while, you'll get one that nothing is right for, but if he ever calls again, you'll remember to not have an opening for him.

# Chet Morris's Stories

## Pelican Story

*Chet was mating for his uncle, Louis Davis, when this story took place.*

We had a hunting party on this slick calm day in the Alligator River, and these two pelicans lit in the decoys and would not leave. We tried hollering at them and waving our arms, but they just wouldn't leave. An unnamed member of our party decided to take one of our rocks we had in the boat for training dogs and throw it at the pelicans to get them to leave. Just trying to get close to them, he got a little *too* close and hit the pelican upside the head and knocked him out cold. He didn't move for a few minutes, and we just knew he had killed him and that the game warden was going to stop by and see a dead pelican in the decoys. Thank God, he suddenly got his act together and wobbled around and eventually flew off. Talk about a relief! Now every time we see a pelican, we tell everyone, "Don't throw anything at it!"

## Mating for Louis

During the 2009–2010 hunting season, when I was mating for Louis Davis, we had a three man hunting party. The wind and weather was going to be perfect for hunting in the lower Alligator River in his twenty-three-foot Parker with the scissor rig.

## Another Breed of Currituck Duck Hunters

Pelicans landing in the decoys on Alligator River. *Courtesy of Chet Morris.*

Chet Morris and his other granddaddy, Carl Davis, in Louis Davis's float blind. *Courtesy of Chet Morris.*

# Fresh Tales from a Native Gunner

We had gotten tied out with a light southwest wind and were killing a handful of ducks. Around nine o'clock, we saw the sky to the west looking ugly and called Kent Vaughn (one of our friends who guides out of Columbia, North Carolina) and asked him what the weather was doing over there.

He said, "It looks a little ugly and is starting to sprinkle, but it's not supposed to last long." We figured we would wait it out because everyone had rain gear, and we were killing ducks. Five minutes before it was too late, Kent called us back and said, "Get outta there!" We started taking everything down in a hurry. Within five minutes, the wind had shifted northwest and was blowing over 40 miles per hour. Where we were, you did not want to see northwest at that speed. The swells got so bad so fast that they did everything but beat us out of the blind. We started picking up decoys and Louis told all the sportsmen, "Sit down, hold on and don't move!" Normally, the captain hooks the seventy-five decoys with the boat hook and slings them to the mate to stack in the bow of the boat. He was doing all he could to keep the boat right in the three-foot swells without running over the decoy lines because that would be a terrible situation. I was very capable of hooking and stacking by myself. The only difficulty was trying to stay on my knees so I wouldn't fall overboard. There were several times when we got side to the waves, and the boat would list so bad the washboards would hit the water. One of the sportsmen wouldn't stay seated and insisted on helping hook the decoys no matter how many times Louis would tell him to sit down. Louis finally realized the man was not going to sit down, so every time he tried to hook a decoy, Louis would grab the man's belt so he wouldn't fall overboard.

We finally got all the decoys up, and I managed to straddle my way to the bow to pick up the headboard of the scissor rig so we could get out of there. We got the rig on and pulled the anchor and rode over to get in the lee of the wind and rain because it was raining so hard it felt like shards of glass were hitting your face. We anchored and looked up to see two twenty-foot waterspouts going through the spot we'd just been in. Louis and I looked at each other at the same time and said, "Holy s——!" The weather passed after an hour, and we all went home safely. From that day on, anybody that gets a call that says the weather's coming—no matter if it is sunny, slick calm and you are killing ducks—you LEAVE!

# Frank Helms

Frank Helms, better known as Frankie, has lived in Currituck all his life. His daddy and mother, Jack and Martha Kay Helms, ran a store in Jarvisburg, North Carolina, and lived in the back part of the store. The store is still there, but has been converted into a restaurant called BJ's Restaurant. Frankie has two older sisters, Sharon and Jackie. I knew them better than I knew Frankie until ten or fifteen years ago. The girls hung out with my daughters and were at our house a lot.

The Helmses' store was the gathering place for the local hunters and fisherman. If you didn't hunt or fish, you didn't fit in. Listening to these guys is what Frankie grew up around.

A couple of the men who hung out at the store were John Wright Jr. and Charlie Dozier. John Jr. was a farmer and manager of Dews Island Club. Charlie was a farmer and duck hunter. They were the best of friends in the summer, but come duck season, they were like the Hatfields and McCoys: dire enemies. I was friends with both of them. I was in the long-distance trucking business at the time and hauled produce for both of them.

There was a dock out in front of Dews Island Club. John Jr. fed the geese there, and there were usually geese hanging around there. Charlie Dozier had a little speed boat. One day, I was riding with Charlie and he ran that boat right up to the dock and whipped her right around, just flying, and the geese took off in a high state of alarm. I put my head down quick. I didn't want John Jr. to see me.

# Fresh Tales from a Native Gunner

Frank Helms in one of his duck blinds. *Courtesy of Frank Helms.*

One more story about those two: Dews Island is separated from John Jr.'s landing (the mainland) by Deep Creek. The creek is about one hundred and fifty feet wide at this point. Mr. Thurmond Chatham, who owned Dews Island, had a walk bridge built across Deep Creek. It was a humpback bridge because he couldn't block navigable waters; boats had to be able to get under it. Charlie's gas boat would just barely get under it, so he put a windshield on top of the cabin so he couldn't get under it. He did this so John Jr. would have to put a draw in the bridge! You had to pull it up with a block and tackle.

John Jr. would never sell the owners of Dews Island a right-of-way to the island. That's called job security. Without going over his land, their only access was by water.

Some others who hung around Jack Helms's store were Roy Sawyer, Herbert Lee Waterfield and Nathan Cartwright Jr.

Now back to Frankie. I called up Frankie and told him I was writing a book about the younger breed of hunters. Frankie is fifty-two now (in 2012).

On the appointed date, he invited me to go down to his house and eat supper with him and his wife, Brenda. When I got there, they were baking

# Another Breed of Currituck Duck Hunters

It's not just men and boys who duck hunt in Currituck—women duck hunt too, including Frank Helms's daughter, Hollie, pictured here. *Courtesy of Frank Helms.*

ducks that were just about ready to come out of the oven. I think Frankie was the cook because Brenda doesn't like ducks. She had chicken. I'm sure Brenda fixed the sweet potatoes, wild rice, pasta, bread and brownies we had to go with it. I want to add that Frankie is a good cook as well as a good guide. Nowadays, the young boys just breast the ducks. They don't pick and bake the whole duck like people used to do. Until a few years ago, I'd never eaten ducks cooked any way except baked.

After supper, we got down to talking about duck hunting. Frankie's property is on the north side of a canal that goes into Dews Quarter Bay, and Charlie Dozier's property is on the south side of the canal. Frankie has a boat basin on his side of the canal, and Charlie has one on his side. Charlie had a boat shed on his side which is still there.

I told Frankie that driving up to his house had brought back a lot of memories. I could see Charlie's boat basin across the canal. In the 1960s, I used to keep my gas boat and float rig at Charlie's when the ducks were in the south end of the sound. I always went where the most ducks were using.

Sometimes I kept the rig in the canal right in front of Walnut Island Restaurant when the ducks were using south of the Narrows and north of Dews Island. Can you imagine leaving a rig there now with two hundred wood

# Fresh Tales from a Native Gunner

Ditch or canal from Frank Helms's and Charlie Dozier's landing to Dews Quarter Bay. *Courtesy Frank of Helms.*

ducks and ninety canvas geese in it? We ate breakfast at Walnut Island, so this was real convenient. I kept my rig at Jones Dock in Waterlily most of the time.

Frankie told me he got his first shotgun when he was six years old. It was a single barrel 410. His daddy and Roy Sawyer started taking him hunting when he was young.

I asked Frankie when he started guiding. He said he started on weekends guiding at Dews Island for John Wright Jr. when he was fifteen years old, and did that until he was seventeen. Then he moved away for one winter. He went to Houston, Texas. Then he came back to Currituck and guided for Colon Grandy until 1989, when he started Frank's Guide Service. He ran that for two years, then ran the Brinson Landing Hunt Club for three years. That was at the end of Snow's Lane in Powell's Point. It had twelve members from the western part of North Carolina. After that, he started guiding full time for himself. His people used to stay at the Riviera and Walnut Island Motels. Now most of them stay at the Holiday Inn Express in Kitty Hawk, and all of them meet him in the morning at the 7-Eleven in Grandy for coffee. From there, they split up to go with his different guides.

Ryan Kight and Justin Thomas, guides for Frank Helms. *Courtesy of Frank Helms.*

I asked how many blinds he was using. He said right now he is using fourteen. He has three in Dare County, six on the east side of Currituck Sound and five on the west side down the shoreline from his house.

Frankie has made his whole living on the water; hunting, fishing, and crabbing. He said his mama remembered that when he was six years old and in the first grade, he came home from that first day of school and told her there wasn't any need for him to go to school because he wasn't going to do anything but hunt and fish.

As much time as he has spent on the water, there must be some bad experiences Frankie could tell about. I asked him, and he said most of the really bad times were before they had decent boats. He said that one October season, he and Mike Mercer were right down the shore from Currituck Club. They were in a twelve-foot Sears & Roebuck boat. The wind was blowing 70 miles per hour. It blew the boat over the top of the boat hide. They had to chase it down the marsh five or six hundred yards, swimming part of the

# Fresh Tales from a Native Gunner

*Right*: Joe Schwin Jr. from Hickory, North Carolina. *Courtesy of Frank Helms.*

*Below*: Joe Schwin Sr. from Hickory, North Carolina, with teal, canvasback and widgeon. *Courtesy of Frank Helms.*

## Another Breed of Currituck Duck Hunters

Bryan Palmer, Barrell Rice and Randy from Petersburg, Virginia. *Courtesy of Frank Helms.*

Frank Helms, Terry Smith and his son from Rocky Mount, North Carolina. *Courtesy of Frank Helms.*

# Fresh Tales from a Native Gunner

time, to get the boat. It was blowing so hard it was spinning the little boat around like a top, and they couldn't get it back to the blind until the wind slacked up. This was in 1976 or 1977.

He said he'd lost a lot of his clients from age. I asked where most of his hunters came from. He said most come from North Carolina, South Carolina and Virginia. He now has a lot of people coming from Pennsylvania. They can kill ducks up there but not the variety they can kill here. They want something to mount. He said they were good people, easy to get along with. If they come down here and kill six or seven ducks, they are happy.

Frankie said his best memories are of hunting with his daddy and his friends. He said he could still see it in his eyes, going across the sound in a sixteen-foot juniper skiff with a 40-horsepower Mercury outboard motor. That was the standard hunting boat then. There were ducks everywhere, and his daddy was cussing because there weren't any ducks.

He said John Jr.'s boys didn't care much about hunting and that John Jr. and Roy Sawyer would take him hunting with them a lot.

Boys from South Carolina with swan. *Courtesy Frank Helms.*

Hall Rouse from the Raleigh, North Carolina area. *Courtesy of Frank Helms.*

In 1977, Jack and Martha Kay Helms sold the store and built a house on North River. Jack went to work at Dews Island as Assistant Manager under John Wright Jr. and worked there for ten years. During the hunting season, they stayed at the island. Martha Kay cooked and Jack guided. After that, Jack fished with Frankie until Jack died.

The biggest change in hunting bush and point blinds in Currituck is the type of boats used. It used to be sixteen-foot juniper skiffs, but then it was either a sixteen-foot fiberglass Sea Ox, an eighteen-foot Sea Hawk or an eighteen-foot Parker or Maycraft. When Sea Ox came out with a twenty-foot boat, Frankie said it looked as big as a barge. He now hunts in a twenty-three-foot boat.

Billy Ferrell was the first guide who helped Frankie, but he's gone on to a steady job. Justin Thomas is the one who helps Frankie year round now.

# Fresh Tales from a Native Gunner

Frank Helms tying out at a point blind in Dew's Quarter Bay. *Courtesy of Frank Helms.*

Frank Helms bringing in a swan. *Courtesy of Frank Helms.*

Frank Helms with his grandson, Luke. I thought I started my grandsons out early when they killed their first duck at seven years old. Luke killed his first duck at four years old! *Courtesy of Frank Helms.*

Others who have guided for him at times are Mike Mercer, Thomas Newbern, Paul Vance and my grandsons, Chandler Sawyer and Chet Morris, who helped him a little this year when Louis Davis didn't have anything for them.

Sometimes he has four or five rigs out, but most of the time he tries to keep two rigs busy.

*You can get in touch with Frankie by writing to Frank Helms, PO Box 244, Jarvisburg, NC, 27947, or by calling 252-491-8310. His email address is: franksguides@ embarqmail.com*

# Barry Walker

Barry is not a float blind hunter, but he has a good blind on a point of marsh and is guaranteed to entertain you. He is retired now from the Forestry Service.

He lives in Grandy and started guiding part time when he was twenty-three years old. Ralph Saunders's hunting lodge was right down the road from Barry's house, and if Ralph was short a guide, he'd call Barry. Barry didn't get paid overtime from the Forestry Service, but he got compensation time and earned a lot of it. He'd take that time plus his vacation time during hunting season until he retired.

Early on, Barry didn't have a blind of his own, but Ralph would let him use one of his, and he kinda taught him what to do. Barry also helped Ralph build his blinds.

I wrote about Ralph Saunders in my third book, *Currituck: Ducks, Politics & Outlaw Gunners*. What used to be Ralph's lodge is now the clubhouse for Goose Creek Golf Club. When Ralph stopped running the hunting lodge, he let Barry have his blind at Red Head Point. This blind had been, Ellie Saunders's, Ralph's daddy. This is a good location and has been hunted many a year.

Barry has two juniper skiffs that his cousin, Newton Hampton, built for him. Bruce Bess fiberglassed them for him. The skiff he goes back and forth to the blind in is wide, was built in 1980 and is about sixteen feet long. His decoy skiff is about sixteen feet and was built in 1984. He has a double skiff

# Another Breed of Currituck Duck Hunters

Barry Walker in his sixteen-foot juniper skiff that his cousin, Newton Hampton, built for him in 1980. He puts a spray hood on it in the winter. *Courtesy of Barry Walker.*

Barry's blind at Redhead Point in Currituck Sound. *Courtesy of Barry Walker.*

# Fresh Tales from a Native Gunner

hide at his blind. He leaves the decoy skiff there all season. The skiff he goes back and forth in has a spray hood on it that Larry Brown built for him. Larry has built several spray hoods for me and does a good job.

When Barry was hunting for Ralph, he kept his boat at Ralph and Wendell Barco's landing. After Ralph quit hunting, that property was sold. Now Barry keeps his boat in a canal at Waterview Shores in Grandy. The canal goes right into Dowdy's Bay, which is a protected place to keep his boat and is a shorter run to his blind. If it's not rough, he can make the run to his blind in twelve to eighteen minutes, but if you get caught out there in a blow, it can take forty-five minutes to an hour to get back.

Most of Barry's men stay at the beach. Some stay at Midway Marina because that's a lot closer and because it's easy to get an early breakfast at Kevin's Store.

Barry talked some about his wife Nancy's grandfather, Harrison Midgett. Barry said he loved to talk to him because he'd tell him about market hunting and had all kinds of stories. Mr. Midgett was born on Hatteras Island in Chicamacomico, now Rodanthe, in 1889. When he was a young boy, his family moved to Currituck. He told Barry about market hunting in battery rigs with live decoys. They would take the ducks to Newbern's Landing, where they were put in barrels that were packed with ice and loaded on freight boats to go to Norfolk. From there, they would be loaded on a train and shipped up north. They mainly went to New York. He worked with the Wright Brothers of Jarvisburg for many years and said he really thought a lot of them. He share cropped in the early years, but that didn't pan out too well. Then he just became a professional guide for the rest of his life as long as he was able to.

Mr. Midgett worked with John Wright Jr. as a guide at Dews Island for the Chathams and Haneses for many years. Besides being an expert hunting and fishing guide, he was a great story teller. Barry said after he got too old to guide, they'd sometimes get him to go along with them fishing just to sit and talk to them.

Mr. Midgett told Barry if he was ever in the sound and there was so much ice he couldn't get a hole to tie his decoys out in to just go in the marsh with a hatchet and chop six or seven chunks of marsh grass and throw them out on the ice.

Barry said he went over to his blind one day when everything was frozen around the marsh, and he decided to try that. He got his hatchet out and chopped up several chunks of marsh and threw them out on the ice. He sat there two or three hours, and nothing happened. "Well, maybe I better do something else," he said. About the time he stepped over the back of the boat to wade out and break some ice, he looked up and a Black Duck was hovering over one of those chunks of ice. He said they killed eight ducks over that stuff. When they killed a duck, they just let him lay there as a decoy. He said it was the most fun he'd had in a long time. When he left there that day, he looked back, and it did look like ducks sitting on the ice. Besides that, the mud that had spattered on the ice looked like duck crap.

He just had one man that day, and he said he really had a ball. Like he said, some days you can go out there with a pretty stand of decoys and you can't get a duck to come close to you. Of course, that cold weather has a lot to do with it, too.

Barry said he thought we just couldn't get many new ducks to come down here this year (2011–2012). The same ducks stayed here, and they got blind-shy and just wouldn't come to you.

Barry has a big blind. He has two boxes with the skiff hide in between. One has the north wind to his back and one has the west wind to his back.

Willard Andrews looking out at decoys from Barry Walker's blind. *Courtesy of Barry Walker.*

# Fresh Tales from a Native Gunner

*Right*: Barry Walker cooking a steak on the grill in the blind. *Courtesy of Barry Walker.*

*Below*: Inside Barry Walkers's blind. *Courtesy of Barry Walker.*

63

He has a grill set up in his blind and does a lot of cooking. He said he started doing that when he was working for Ralph Barco. If nothing else, it broke the monotony. The guys liked hot dogs and hamburgers better than cold sandwiches. They gave the sandwiches to his dog.

Barry said he had one old boy from Richmond, Virginia, who hunted with him and that he'd bring back-fin crabmeat and ribs when he came. He said he remembered one time while he was sitting there eating crabmeat that he looked all around and said, "If those ducks will just leave me alone while I'm eating."

Barry was telling me about one time when Tommy Brock from Elizabeth City was with him, and it was blowing a gale and freezing. Barry said, "We need to wait until the sun comes up so I can see." But Tommy said, "You know them ducks are going to be flying."

"Man I don't know, but all right. I ain't never balked but three times," Barry said. They got about half way across the sound, and the seas were breaking across the spray hood, throwing water in the back of the boat. Barry's raincoat was a solid sheet of ice. Tommy was back there trying to

Don Shaffner from Winston Salem, North Carolina, and Barry Walker. *Courtesy of Barry Walker.*

# Fresh Tales from a Native Gunner

Tommy Brock and Barry Walker. Tommy was from Elizabeth City, North Carolina, and hunted with Barry a lot. He drowned in a hunting accident on the Pasquotank River when a canoe turned over. *Courtesy of Barry Walker.*

bail, and it was freezing before he could get it out. About this time, Tommy said, "Man, we've screwed up! Turn around!"

"I ain't turning around and letting them sea's come in the back of this boat," Barry said.

When they finally got to the blind, the zipper on Barry's raincoat was frozen and wouldn't work. He couldn't get the coat off, and he got sort of claustrophobic and ripped the zipper out. He tied out the decoys and got the skiff about halfway in the skiff hide when he heard *BAM! BAM! BAM!* He had to go back out and pick up ducks. Barry said, "Wait, I want to shoot some too." He had a full-length beard at the time and said it was frozen solid. They had a good shoot. The story was really funny the way Barry told it, but I had to clean it up some to print it.

One morning, when he was working with Ralph Barco, they went out when he said he told them they had no business going. The sound was frozen up north and the tide was real low, so they went up by Long Point.

Ralph had a boat load and he was leading. Barry was in the middle and Randy Barco was behind him. They were all three going together. They couldn't get up through Jarvis Channel, so Ralph turned and went through the Little Narrows. The tide was rolling through there, and chunks of ice were hitting the boat and knocking it sideways. Ralph's hat brim had an inch of ice on it. His eyelids were frozen open and he couldn't close them. They finally made it to Poplar Branch Landing. "What are you gonna do?" Ralph asked.

"I'm gonna' call my wife and tell her to come get my ass and bring my trailer. I'm gonna carry my rig home," Barry said. He said those boys with him told him, "The next time you say 'we better not go,' we ain't going!" The ice in the upper part of the sound was coming down, the tide was dropping and that ice was boiling through the Narrows.

We got to talking about blue peters (coots). Two years ago, Barry was sitting there in the blind and fell asleep. The man with him punched him and pointed to the skiff hide. There were about two hundred blue peters right in the skiff hide! Barry yelled, "Where in hell did they come from?!" They had swum around the marsh and swam right in there. This year, he was sitting there with the same man. "Uh oh," he heard the man say. He looked up, and about fifty blue peters were swimming right down to them.

Blue peters are good if you skin them. My grandmother used to fry them and make gravy and biscuits. They were *really* good.

When I was a young boy I had an old flat bottom gas boat with a Model A Ford motor in it. If Granny wanted a mess of blue peters, I'd take that gas boat in Coinjock Bay and make a circle or two around a little bunch of Peters to get them in a tight knot. Then I'd get upwind of them, push the throttle wide open on the old A and come downwind on them and shoot a time or two and pick up all I wanted. It wasn't legal, but there weren't many game wardens around then and most everybody did it.

Barry and I got to talking about Coinjock Bay. He was raised up there at Maple. Barry and Carlton Ballance were good friends. Carlton's daddy, Olie, had a blind up there in the northern head of the Bay. He was also a farmer and had a grain bin of corn. The Bay was full of canvasback. Carlton would go up to the grain bin and get some corn and keep that blind baited, and the canvasback would pour in there. Even on a pretty, sunny day they'd pour right in there. He said one foggy day it was right still, not a ripple on the water, and they kept hearing all this splashing in the water and didn't know what it was. When the fog lifted, canvasback were all around the blind.

## Fresh Tales from a Native Gunner

They were about thirteen or fourteen years old when they killed a Widgeon up there one day and didn't know what he was. All they'd ever seen up there were canvasback, redheads, blackheads and blue peters.

Barry served on the Currituck County Game Commission for eight years. He said he had always heard you could mess with another man's wife but you better not mess with his duck blind. I've always heard that saying, too.

*You can reach Barry Walker by writing to him at 6534 Caratoke Highway, Grandy, NC 27939, or you can call him at 252-453-2582.*

# Aaron Mathews

Aaron is thirty years old now (in 2012). He owns a guiding service now in its eight year. He calls himself the "Outfitter." He says he is a fourth-generation guide. He is the only guide I know of who does a combination duck and deer hunt. They duck hunt in the morning and deer hunt in the afternoon. He has a scissor float blind rig, but mostly hunts point blinds. He has a point blind in Piney Island Bay and one or two in Coinjock Bay.

I would say that Aaron specializes in hunting swan and snow geese, mainly in fields. He has several thousand acres of farmland that he has permission to hunt on in Currituck, Camden and Pasquotank Counties.

I asked him to tell me about a typical snow goose hunt. He said he would get up about 3:00 a.m. and meet his men at the motel about 3:30. They usually stay at Midway Marina. They stop at 7-Eleven, the only place open at that time of morning, and get coffee and doughnuts and such. Kevin's Store, where you can get good sandwiches with eggs, bacon, sausage or ham and other things, doesn't open until 4:30 a.m.

Aaron is usually in the field putting out decoys at about 4:00 a.m. They put out anywhere from 800 to 1,200 decoys. He uses full bodies, shells and white rags. It depends on the conditions. If it rains the night before and he can't get the four-wheeler in the field, he uses all rags. It takes about an hour and a half to set up the decoys.

# Fresh Tales from a Native Gunner

Young boy and his dad hunting in Aaron's blind on Eldon Jones's marsh on Coinjock Bay in 2005. *Courtesy of Aaron Mathews.*

Aaron, Christian Johnson and Kenny Rose. *Courtesy of Aaron Mathews.*

# Another Breed of Currituck Duck Hunters

This young boy was a son of the sportsman with snow geese. *Courtesy of Aaron Mathews.*

Emily and her dad, Guber Shane, with Dustin Mathews, Jeremy Evans, Aaron Mathews and his wife, Kristan. Emily and her dad were here from Michigan to film a TV show, *Benielli Bird Hunter. Courtesy Aaron Mathews.*

# Fresh Tales from a Native Gunner

Aaron Mathews with "Go Devil." This is an air-cooled motor. It has a long shaft with a propeller on the end that will run in just enough water to float the boat. *Courtesy of Aaron Mathews.*

For the conservation snow goose season, they can take the plugs out of their guns and use electronic callers. It takes a little extra time to set up the callers. He uses two callers and six speakers.

For a swan hunt, he meets his men at about 4:30 a.m. They make their 7-Eleven stop and are in the field at about 5:00 a.m. He uses thirty swan decoys when he does a swan hunt. Sometimes, he also uses white rags. They wear white Tyvek suites and lay right in the decoys. They do that for both swan and snow goose hunts. A swan hunt usually lasts no longer than two hours and is easy to go to.

If Aaron's duck hunting, and somebody in the party has a swan permit and a swan comes in, of course they can kill him, but he mostly field hunts for swan. In the field, he can take up to ten or fifteen hunters. The farms he hunts on are in Moyock, around Hale's Lake in Camden County, and a few are outside Elizabeth City.

Aaron won the world swan calling contest in Washington, North Carolina, three times. He said most of his hunters come from the Raleigh, Durham, and the Charlotte area. Some come from Fayetteville and Wilmington. He does have hunters that come from New York, New Jersey, Pennsylvania, California, Wyoming, South Carolina and Missouri.

*If you want to get in touch with Aaron you can write to him at PO Box 32, Aydlett, North Carolina, 27916, or call him at 252-619-2880.*

# Dennis Lee Newbern

Dennis Lee comes from an old Jarvisburg, North Carolina family, who has for generations farmed and duck hunted in Currituck County.

Dennis is the oldest of three boys born to Nicholas and Patsy Walker Newbern. The other two boys are Danny, who crabs and has the seafood market in Duck, and Andy. Andy has worked for the Slick family for many years and still manages Narrows Island for them. Until this interview with Dennis, Andy was the only one of the boys I really knew. I knew Andy from seeing him at Narrows Island, and he is on the Whalehead Preservation Trust with me. Now to my conversation with Dennis.

We started talking about Bill Riddick. Dennis's daddy, Nicholas Newbern, hunted with him a lot. I also hunted with Bill Riddick; he is in some of my books. I'd help him take sportsmen sometimes and sometimes he'd help me.

Anyway, Dennis said they usually hunted south of the Narrows, but on this particular day they were hunting north of the Narrows on the Gull Rock, which is in the middle of Currituck Sound between Waterlily and Corolla. They had Bill Riddick's two-man float box. According to Dennis, "There were enough ducks then that we would take several people and change around in the box, so we'd have enough people for the count to make it worthwhile to tie out that big rig. At the time, the limit on canvasback was three. Canvasback and redheads were mainly what we were shooting."

On this day they didn't have sportsmen. They were just hunting for themselves. They had two local men, Newton Hampton and Graham

# Fresh Tales from a Native Gunner

Dennis Lee Newbern farms and duck hunts, as his family has for generations. He also deer and turkey hunts. *Courtesy of Dennis Lee Newbern.*

Keaton, who were farmers and duck hunters. Dennis was only fourteen years old at the time. They just let him tag along for the count.

Dennis said he and his daddy were in the box. His daddy had a twelve gauge Remington Sportsman, and Dennis had a twenty gauge. Somehow, the cap on the end of the forestock of his daddy's gun came off and the big spring in there sprung overboard (I knew what he was doing. He was taking the plug out of his gun so it would hold five shells). They were just standing up to wave for the gas boat when six pintails had their wings set to come in to the decoys. Dennis reached for his gun, but it was gone. His daddy had already grabbed it and started shooting them. He said his daddy knew Dennis wasn't going to kill any of them anyway. We didn't usually get pintails in the middle of the sound. You killed them around the marsh.

Down at Currituck Sports this morning, I was telling Newton Hampton and Graham Keaton about my conversation with Dennis. Newton said that Dennis's daddy, Nicholas, was a very good shot. Nicholas's uncle, Fred Newbern, hunted with me a lot, and he was the best shot that ever laid in my lay down box. He could shoot from either shoulder.

Another thing that Dennis said happened that day. He and his daddy were in the gas boat with Bill Riddick. Newton and Graham were in the sit up box. They were going up to the box with the gas boat and were about a hundred yards from them when seven geese came by them, low on the water, and went right in there to the decoys, and they never killed a one.

Dennis said he started guiding as soon as he got out of high school. During the first five years, he guided in the fields on their farm for geese. They seldom hunted on the water. I know that there were a lot of geese in the fields around here then. There were about twenty-five hundred geese that went in my father-in-law's field at Maple every morning.

Dennis said on moonlit nights, they would drive a pick-up truck out in the wheat field to run the geese out to keep them from feeding there all night.

They had a few ponds they hunted, which was pretty much illegal. They never shot them except when the weather was bad, and then only about every other week.

The first five or six years Dennis guided, he took parties for Vern Berg, who lived in Duck Woods but worked out of the Sea Ranch Hotel in Kill Devil Hills. "He'd send people up here and they'd have a great hunt, and the ones they carried down to Dare County around Oregon Inlet weren't killing a thing," Dennis said.

Dennis also said that he once had a group that killed their seven geese and were back at the Sea Ranch by 8:30 a.m. When the group that had been hunting in Dare County came in, they didn't have a thing. They were fit to be tied. Dennis was supposed to be off the next day. Vern told him that if he'd just take this group that had been in Dare County hunting the next morning and let one bunch of geese come to them, he could send them back to the Sea Ranch and pay Dennis for the day. Dennis took them, and they were back to the Sea Ranch at 8:30 that morning with their seven geese. All were happy.

One year, they had the Wiley Leary field up on Poplar Branch Road. Dennis said they'd shoot geese up there a lot and snow geese when they first started coming in the fields around here. One day, four Canada geese came to them in that field. They killed three of them dead and crippled one. They hunted for that cripple for two hours before they finally found him. All of them had neck bands and leg bands on them. They sent the bands in, and it turned out all four of them were banded the year before in the same field

# Fresh Tales from a Native Gunner

they were killed in. They thought they were going to get bands from Canada or somewhere.

When Dennis started duck hunting, Ernest Brickhouse was superintendent of Pine Island Club, and he let them use some blinds in Pine Island Marsh. He said there were more ducks in one bunch than anyone would see all year now. One year, the state estimated there 3,500 Ringnecks in the Petty Pond at Pine Island.

One day in the 1980s, Dennis and a friend were hunting in a Pine Island blind called Bluff Point. It was snowing to beat the band, and a Black Duck came in and lit in the decoys. It was one of those years you couldn't kill a Black Duck until some time in December. The duck kept sitting in the decoys, and they got to looking at him. He had a sprig tail. They'd never seen anything like this on a Black duck. It was about three or four inches long.

Curiosity finally got the best of them, and Dennis decided to shoot him and see what it was. The sprig turned out to be the antenna for a radio transmitter that was on her back, and there was a battery pack secured with a harness around her wing.

Dennis carried it home and put it on the TV. About three weeks later a guy knocked on his door. He said, "I want to talk to you a minute. I'm a biologist and I got nothing to do with anything else. The Black Duck I'm looking for seems to be in there." He had a handheld antenna like people with hunting dogs have. He turned it around and when it was pointed at Dennis's house, it would go *beep, beep, beep*. As soon as he turned it away from the house, the beeping would stop.

"Yeah, I know exactly what you want," Dennis said. It was in a plastic case that had been shot, and Dennis didn't think it was working but it was. The man said he was down there in a plane about two weeks before and got the general area where it was. He said he had found some that had been eaten by animals. They could track it right to the place and pick it up. He said, "I came down here about two weeks ago and your truck was sitting in the yard with three dead Canada geese in the back so I figured I was at the right house." He took the radio transmitter. He actually wanted the duck. Dennis said Graf Beasley cleaned the ducks for them, and Dennis had the duck, but there was no way to tell which one it was.

The man told Dennis they turned loose fifty hen mallards in Delaware with transmitters and that Dennis had killed that duck the next day. That tells you how fast a duck can move if he needs to. Dennis said there were a couple more black ducks with transmitters killed around here that he knew of.

Dennis worked at Dews Island Club for about twenty-five years. He said when he was a little boy, John Wright Jr., who was superintendent of Dews Island Club, would take him and Norman Newbern Jr. on Sunday afternoons, and they would ride around the blinds and dump bags of corn right off the stern of the gas boat. The propeller wash would scatter it. I told him I did the same thing when I was a little boy with Mr. Norman Ballance (who was superintendent of Bells Island Club), and that was a long time before Dennis was born. Mama and daddy would go to Bells Island to visit Mr. Norman and Miss Nell on Sunday afternoons, and I would go with Mr. Norman in the gas boat to feed around the blinds. Incidentally, I own that same gas boat today. It was built by Mr. Pat O'Neal for Bells Island Club in 1947. I plan to give it to The Whalehead Preservation Trust if they ever get anywhere to store and display the old Currituck boats.

When Dennis was a little boy, his daddy, Nicholas Newbern, Floyd Parker and a lot of other people worked at Dews Island Club. Back then the clubs started feeding in October and fed through February. We were able to keep ducks here then.

When Dennis worked at Dews Island, he said they hunted across the sound ninety-nine percent of the time. They had Thanksgiving and Christmas week off when he worked there. They hunted for themselves during that time.

Dews Island had three blinds in the Pine Island Marsh. They were Gourd Island, Shoe Hole and R Cove. After John Wright Jr. died and his son, Jerry, was running the club, Dennis said Jerry would never let them hunt on Dews Island. He said it didn't matter how bad the weather was or how thick the ice was; if Jerry could get over there with the gas boat, they hunted across the sound.

Before Dennis started working at Dews Island, his brother, Danny, also started working there. At that time, Dews Island had use of Brant Island, which belonged to Currituck Shooting Club. When Dennis worked there, they had use of Burris's, which also belonged to Currituck Shooting Club.

Dennis told me some of the best hunts he ever had were in the October season. I told him that when I was running Monkey Island Club (1974–

## Fresh Tales from a Native Gunner

1978), you could go across Currituck Sound and never see a sign of a duck. We had a point blind named Net Scafell that was right near the Monkey Island Club/Whalehead Club property line on Currituck Beach. We had that blind blended in with the marsh so good, I could hardly find it myself in the early morning.

You wouldn't think there was a duck in Currituck, but when they started shooting up the beach in the Hay Ponds on the Swan Island property, those ducks would fly down that beach, and we would have some of the best hunting of the whole hunting season in October, mostly pintails. It was an early morning deal and then it was over with.

Some people have been hunting with Dennis during Thanksgiving and Christmas weeks every year for at least thirty years. They hunted one day this year and saw eight ducks all day long. He said he was talking about near and far. He had the same crew the year before, and they hunted two and a half days and killed over fifty ducks.

Steve Cates from Alamance County, North Carolina, and Donnie Harringer from Burlington, North Carolina, have been hunting with Dennis Lee every Christmas week since the late 1970s. *Courtesy Dennis of Lee Newbern.*

## Another Breed of Currituck Duck Hunters

Dennis has another group from Asheboro, North Carolina, that has hunted with him for about twenty years. They started bringing so much gear with them that he had to quit taking them. Dennis has two sixteen foot juniper skiffs. Joe Hayman made one and Milford Austin the other. What I'm getting at is he doesn't have a real big boat, and there is not room for a whole lot of extra gear. These folks would bring two Dutch ovens, a Coleman stove, coolers and five or six gallons of bottled water. The thing they really did need and never brought was rain gear.

He told them if they ever brought that much stuff again, he was not going to take them anymore. They did, and he hasn't taken them since.

I asked Dennis where most of his people stay. He said most of them stay on the beach. It's not that far back up to his place. He said the biggest question they have is where they can get some breakfast.

When they first started the snow goose season, he said they were so dumb he'd use baby diapers, milk jugs, newspapers or anything white for decoys, but that's changed. He said for the past ten years, you don't stand much of a chance of killing one, and that you stand a better chance of driving your pick-up right out in the field and shooting out the window.

He doesn't understand it. They will go in the same wheat field on their farm for ten days in a row. You can go out there and get in the ditch without building a blind and they know you are there.

He took a party this year and they wouldn't even fly over them. It got to the point where Dennis said he thought they could see the tire tracks in the dew where he was driving in the field! The party stayed until ten thirty, then came in and went to McDonald's for breakfast. They went back to the field, and the geese were sitting there. "As soon as we left," he said, "they went in there. Now how did they know we were not there?" It's gotten to the point, he won't even mess with them anymore.

Dennis keeps his boat at a place Junior Baum had that his grandmother bought on Dews Quarter Bay. He used to keep it at William Earl Wright's because he carried a lot of bass fishermen for him. He said there was one time he fished twenty-eight days straight. He fished out of Mrs. Barrett's then because that is where the people were staying. That's up on Poplar Branch road, the lodge I wrote about in Mark Marshall's story.

For awhile, Dennis fished for Colon Grandy. He said Elmer Merrell and Bootie Spruill were fishing there, too. He said he'd never been so embarrassed in his life. Dennis said they'd come in there with seven- or eight-pound bass every day, and he just had one-and-half- to three-pound fish. He said he learned a lot from Elmer Merrell. They were good friends. He said that, as a woodsman, he didn't know anybody any slicker than Elmer was. He taught Dennis a lot about trapping. He said that when you trap otter, you never set the trap unless it's raining.

Dennis hunted dove and quail a lot with Roy Sawyer. He was the retriever because Roy couldn't walk too well, but he taught him how to mark a bird when he went down. He would line up two places and could pretty much tell you where the bird was.

Dennis said one day that he, Roy Sawyer and Marshall Kight were quail hunting and that Roy would go to pieces when the quail got up. He lost all comprehension of anything else. They got out of the truck and didn't walk forty yards before they had walked right past the quail. The quail got up behind them. Roy turned right around and shot the window out of Marshall's pickup!

Another time they were quail hunting up at Grandy, and the quail were in the yard right beside the house. He knew they were there. They were always there. He told Roy to walk on down past where they were. Dennis was going to run them up, but told Roy not to shoot because there was a house right there about thirty feet from the quail. Dennis got the quail up, and they didn't fly sixty feet. Roy shot and Dennis could hear the shot hitting the house. A lady came tearing out of the house cussing Dennis. He hadn't done anything, but he just had to stand there and take it.

"Well, I didn't shoot them the first time they got up," Roy said. Dennis was innocent, but he had to take the rap for it.

Getting back to where he keeps his boat now, Dennis's family owns about 200 acres north of Dozier's ditch where Frank Helms leaves out of. He said they have a big canal just north of Dozier's ditch with a boathouse. Dennis left from behind Walnut Island Motel for about ten years. Barry Nelms let him leave out of there because some of his people were staying at the motel and they ate in the restaurant.

When Vern Berg at the Sea Ranch Hotel in Kill Devil Hills approached Dennis about taking duck hunters for him, the October season was just starting. "Well, come on and go hunting with me tomorrow and I'll show you where the blinds are," Dennis said.

## Another Breed of Currituck Duck Hunters

"There're no duck out there in the summertime," Berg said,

"Well, you just come on and go with me," Dennis said.

That morning, they were in Pine Island Marsh, and at about nine o'clock, the ducks started coming out of Straight Creek. They were going inside of them, and they weren't getting to shoot them. Berg counted fourteen bunches of Widgeon that morning. They were going north, coming from the south marsh. Nobody was messing with them down there. Vern Berg couldn't believe how many ducks he saw that morning. They only killed three or four mallards.

One day, Dennis took Jim Hunt, the governor, and his grandson. He said Hunt didn't even know how to load the gun. But he was mainly taking Hunt's grandson out to kill a swan. Jim Hunt just went along.

Dennis took some guys and their Pentecostal Holiness minister several times. The preacher wanted to kill a swan, so one year he got a swan permit. They were out there in the blind, and it wasn't too long before an old swan came flapping along. He was kinda coming around from behind them. The preacher jumped up and *BAM! BAM! BAM!*

"GD, I can't believe I missed him!"

It wasn't an hour later before he started drinking. Then they started calling him the cussing and drinking preacher. The next go 'round, he got his swan.

Dennis was just a young boy when all the canvasback were here. This was the late 1960s. He said there were three blinds tied out back there on Dews Quarter Bay. One was in Mr. Charlie Wright's pond, there was the one Dennis and his daddy were in and then there was next blind down. Snookie Wright was in one and Bill Riddick was in one.

He said they shot and shot. When they came in, they only had three ducks that were legal. Dennis said he had a 410. He was just there.

Charlie Dozier came out of Dozier's ditch with a gas boat. Snookie had gone out to get a duck and the motor had conked out. He was out there with a whole bunch of ducks he didn't need in the boat! Here came that boat toward him. Snookie was pulling the starter cord on the motor with one hand, poling with the other hand and looking back at that boat. His daddy and whoever else was with them were about to die laughing at him because they knew it was Charlie.

I told Dennis I could tell him a story about that. I had my float rig tied out north of Dews Island and out from Ralph Barco's landing in that deep water. I had Fred Newbern (Dennis's great uncle), Baxter Williams, Vernon Lee Creekmore and Robert Balance with me.

We used to buy decoy weights by the dozen from Sanders Company in Elizabeth City, and a dozen would come wired together. I had a dozen in the gas boat. We had too many canvasback, so we had tied the extra ones to the duck weights. All but Robert Ballance were going to get in the skiff and take the rig up. Fred told Robert, "If I turn my cap around, drop those ducks overboard."

Well, we hadn't been taking up the decoys too long before we saw this fast white outboard boat with a windshield and canopy on top pop around the north end of Dews Island and head right for us. We thought it was the game warden. Fred started spinning his hat around. When the boat got up to us, it turned out to be Charlie Dozier. Fred said, "Robert, you didn't drop those ducks overboard did you?" Fred asked.

"Yeah. You told me if you turned your cap around to drop them overboard and you were just spinning your cap around!" Robert said. Fred laid words on Robert because we couldn't get the ducks back.

Dennis said some of the first duck hunting he ever did was in some blinds that used to belong to Mr. Dexter Snow south of Web Marsh. He had three blinds down there. He had given them to his two sons. Jarvis had two, and Julian had one.

I wrote about Mr. Dexter Snow in my fourth book, *Untold Stories of Old Currituck Duck Clubs*. He was superintendent of Whalehead Club while Mr. Ray Adams owned it, and before that, he hauled moonshine from East Lake to Snow's Landing. Dennis's grandmother was Mr. Dexter Snow's daughter.

Now back to hunting.

Jarvis always let Dennis use his two blinds, and they were always particular about their landing road. He could understand that, not wanting to get the road messed up. They had a locked gate he had to go through. Dennis said even when he was small that there were hardly ever any ducks down there.

Once in a while, there would be a few around Web Marsh if somebody was taking care of it. I'm sure you know what I mean.

One day, he had two sportsmen in the Jarvis blind. Seven canvasback lit in the decoys, and they had two blackheads with them. It was not legal to shoot canvasback at that time. They were getting right to shoot the blackheads when all the canvasback dove. They shot and killed the blackheads. They were the only two ducks they killed that day.

Dennis heard some talking when he went out to start taking up the decoys. He looked back, and the federal game warden had come out of the marsh. He beckoned to Dennis to come up there. He went up to the marsh, and the warden said, "I've been watching you for several hours. Why didn't you shoot those canvasback?"

"Because it's not legal to shoot them," Dennis said.

The warden asked to see his hunting license and duck stamp. He looked at it and said, "You haven't signed it." Dennis said, "No, I collect them and I haven't signed it." It was sprinkling rain. The Warden pulled a pen out of his pocket and told Dennis to sign it. Then he asked Dennis if he'd give him a ride back to the landing. "No," Dennis told him, "walk back out like you came in."

When Dennis got back to the landing, there were more game wardens there. They went through all their gear and the boat, but all they had were those two blackheads.

About three days later, he got a ticket in the mail for not having his duck stamp signed. I think he said that cost him $50!

When the tide is real low at Snow's Landing, there are a lot of five gallon liquor jugs on the bottom. You have to be careful walking there because many of them are broken.

I wrote in one of my other books that when they came in from East Lake with a load of moonshine and if the cars were not at the landing to take it to Virginia, they would run a line through the finger holes of the five gallon jugs and put them overboard. The purpose of the line was so they could find them.

He was telling me about one time when the sound was frozen over. This must have been in the late 1970s. When it started thawing up and the ice started piling up on blinds like icebergs, he said he and a friend made it across the sound. They didn't take anything to hunt with. They just had one gun and seven shells. They got in a blind and killed six ducks and one goose with their seven shells.

One time when he was hunting out of Walnut Island, he had two men from Minnesota. The sound was frozen, but they said that didn't matter to them. They were used to ice.

They broke out to an open water blind, and he beat out a hole and pushed the ice under the ice enough to tie out a few decoys. It took him an hour or so to do this. Ducks were coming, and they were doing pretty good. Another boat that came out of Walnut Island and was headed for Long Point cut that whole sheet of ice loose. He told the men that boat had cut a hundred acres of ice loose and that they had to go. He went out in the boat and started getting the decoys up. The blind was just quivering. They weren't too alarmed about it. They didn't realize what was about to happen.

Dennis knew better than to go back in that skiff hide. He pulled up alongside the blind and told them to throw him their stuff. They wanted to know why he didn't come in the skiff hide. He told them to just throw their stuff to him. They did, and he managed to get them in the skiff. He said when they got about a hundred feet from the blind, the ice took it all away.

I've always had a lot of respect for ice. When it starts moving, it takes everything in its path. When we just had wood skiffs with no fiberglass, ice would cut the bottom off just like it had been sawed if we ran the skiff through it and window glass ice was the worst.

Kelly and their son, John Hunter Newbern, after a good day's hunt in 2012. Hunter, as he goes by, is a senior in college. *Courtesy of Dennis Lee Newbern.*

Kelly with a wild turkey she killed. She loves turkey and deer hunting as well as duck hunting. *Courtesy of Dennis Lee Newbern.*

In 1983 or '84, Dennis carried three men whose names were George Patten. It was a father, son, and grandson. The father was probably the son of General George Patten of World War II fame.

Dennis Lee said he remembers they were tied out in the open sound and killed fifteen ducks and five geese. They all had gold monogrammed Remington model 1100 shotguns.

I told Dennis Lee that in 1982, when I made my first trip down the Intracoastal Waterway with the Ferrell brothers, there was a sailboat tied up right next to us in Thunderbolt, Georgia. It had several men on it, and one of them said he was General George Patten. They were on their way to the Bahamas.

Dennis Lee Newbern and Kelly have a son, John Hunter Newbern, who is now (in 2012) a senior in college. Kelly loves to hunt, especially deer and turkey, but she also duck hunts. She is a finish carpenter and helps Dennis Lee build his blinds.

Dennis Lee Newbern is a colorful character who tells it like it is, and I thoroughly enjoyed talking to him.

# James Guard

James Guard comes from an old Currituck family. His granddaddy, John Guard Sr., ran a store at Poplar Branch and built boats. The ones I know of were flat-bottom gas boats with box tunnels in them. This was so they would run in shallow water, and there is plenty of that around Poplar Branch. His daddy was John Guard Jr. He farmed and guided full time in the hunting season.

James said he remembered his granddaddy building two gas boats at the same time. One was for Purnell Griggs, and the other was for Rupert Parker. He said he remembers it because he jumped off one of them on to a board with a nail in it that went clean through his foot. He said the worst part of it was when they poured kerosene on it. I remember when they used to pour kerosene on a cut or puncture wound.

James started hunting when he was five years old. He said they had him wrapped up in an old raincoat. He killed his first goose when he was six years old.

James said his daddy was an excellent shot. He didn't tell me if he inherited that ability or not, but his daughter, Amy, did. He said she is an excellent shot and hunts with him a lot.

He has two blinds that have been in his family for several generations. He has one at Hog Island, which is 1,250 yards west of the Currituck Shooting Club dock. The one he hunts mostly is in the Big Narrows at what they call the South Mouth. Where the blind is, the water is shallow and the bottom is hard. He can hunt there when it's blowing hard and it doesn't get too rough.

# Another Breed of Currituck Duck Hunters

James Guard and his granddaughter, Maggie Blankenship, in a duck blind in Currituck Sound. *Courtesy of Andy Blankship.*

A flat bottom box tunnel gas boat built by John Guard Sr. and used at Currituck Shooting Club. It was in a boathouse at Walnut Island. Some lady gave it to Levie Bunch Jr. He gave it to Wilson Snowden for the boat museum we are trying to get for old Currituck boats. They brought it up here and put it under my shelter. *Author's collection.*

## Fresh Tales from a Native Gunner

James started guiding when he was thirteen years old. He guided some people that his daddy had guided for years. He said people would come back year after year and book for a week at a time. He guided for Miss Elsie Jackson. The hunters roomed and boarded with her.

I asked James where most of his sportsmen come from and he said they come from all over. Two come from New York. When James was thirteen years old, he was running a gas boat pulling a skiff across the sound to the blinds. That's what everybody did then. This was before the big fiberglass Sea Ox, Sea Hawk, Parker, May Craft and other boats with big outboards. You anchored the gas boat off from the blind and left it there until you got ready to go back home. You used the skiff with a little outboard motor if you had one; if not, you just had a shoving pole to use around the blind.

## Amy's First Hunt

They had a pair of pintails come up. He missed his and she knocked hers out. They looked all around the blind and couldn't find him. He got out in

James Guard and his daughter, Amy Blankenship, in his blind in the South Mouth of the Big Narrows in Currituck Sound. *Courtesy of Andy Blankenship.*

the boat and circled the blind about twice. The duck had hit right on the back of the blind in the bushes. He was sitting right there watching them. That started a fiasco. When James started to back up to get him, the duck jumped overboard. They had the dog in the boat and she decided she was going overboard. They couldn't shoot the cripple because the dog was right on top of him. Then he got a decoy line wrapped in the propeller. James was real excited because he didn't want his daughter to lose her first duck. It turned out he didn't have to worry about that. The dog got the duck! Amy was a senior in high school at that time.

James's friend, Jim Isley from Clemmons, North Carolina, who he has been carrying hunting since 1969, likes for Amy to hunt with him and James. One day, they had left the blind to take the dog to the marsh. When they came back, Amy had three ducks in the water.

James was a schoolteacher for thirty-one years. During that time, he could only hunt on Saturdays and during Thanksgiving and Christmas holidays. He said he liked to see it snow because the school would let out. He'd be out of the schoolyard before the school buses.

Jim Isley, James Guard's longtime friend from Clemmons, North Carolina, in a duck blind in Currituck Sound. *Courtesy of Andy Blankenship.*

# Fresh Tales from a Native Gunner

In 1976, we had a real cold winter. Currituck Sound froze over solid. The school ran out of heating oil and they had to close the school. James said that as soon as they said school was out, he took off. He got a friend, and they put some decoys in an aluminum skiff. Each had a pitchfork. They took off to a blind where they made an ice hole. He said you could shove that skiff over the ice with those pitchforks about as fast as you could run.

He saw one of the members of his church one day. The man said, "You ain't gonna believe what I saw the other day. Two fools with pitch forks were shoving a skiff across the ice to go hunting!"

"Yeah, folks are crazy about hunting!" James said. Later he told the man who it was.

## Just Talking About Ducks

James and I were talking about why we don't have many ducks anymore. Everybody has their own opinion about it. James and I agree on what we think are a lot of the reasons.

Fast outboards are one of the main reasons. A duck can't sit down in Currituck Sound. He has to go to an impoundment, a pond in the marsh or go out in Albemarle Sound. Another thing is where most of the ducks that used to come down the Eastern Flyway through Chesapeake Bay and Currituck Sound now go to inland impoundments, farm ponds, and other places. Another reason is the warm winters. The ducks can get plenty of food up north of us and have no reason to come down here. The 2010–2011 season was a good example. When it turned cold up north, the ducks came. We had the most ducks we've had in thirty or forty years that season. We'd get some good shooting, and the ducks would move on south and more would come. Everybody had good shooting. Late in the season most years, the same ducks come and, they've been shot so much in the same place that they know where the blinds are as good as you do.

James said he'd like to see it like it used to be. You couldn't leave the landing until daybreak. We had ducks then. I told him that would suit me fine. When I was hunting with my float box, we never left the landing until day break. You had to see where the ducks were using. You'd see a bunch of ducks and run them up. If they came back, you'd tie there. If they didn't, you went on somewhere else.

He also said he'd get shot for saying it, but that he'd like to see you have to take up by one or two o'clock in the afternoon. I told him that wouldn't bother me either.

You have to take up at 4:20 p.m. in part of Currituck Sound now, and the rest of the Sound is sunset like the federal law. When you start taking up at 4:20, the ducks start to fly about that time. If you start taking up at sunset, the ducks start flying about that time. I don't know how they know, but the ducks know what's going on. It's kinda like Mr. Sam Walker at Poplar Branch used to say: "If you could give a gun to the ducks we'd all be extinct, 'cause they are smarter than we are."

Here's another thing we used to do (don't anybody get any ideas, because we don't do it now): I'd take a bag of corn, lay it up on the stern of the gas boat and let it trickle over. The prop wash would spread it and not too far from the blind.

Another thing Bill Riddick and I used to do out in the open sound was stick a pine bush down and put corn around it. After the ducks got on it,

Andy Blankenship, James's son-in-law, his dog Lucille and James looking for a cripple duck. The day I talked to James and saw Lucille, she was ten years old and looked and acted like she was five, and her coat looked like velvet. In the 2010–11 season, they killed 316 ducks and Lucille retrieved 260 of them. If they killed three ducks out of a bunch in the fast current in the Narrows, by the time she got to the third duck, it had probably drifted 200 yards. *Courtesy of Andy Blankenship.*

we'd move the pine bush and tie our float rig near it. So far as I know, there is nothing illegal about that. We respected one another and wouldn't tie on the other man's corn. I don't think you'd find it to be that way now.

I've heard that people who hunted the same blind everyday over around the marsh would take a fruit jar of corn with them every day. When they got ready to leave that evening, they would spread the jar of corn. That night, the black ducks would eat it up, so he wouldn't have to worry about it being there the next day, but ducks would come back looking for it.

Andy Blankenship is James's son-in-law. The day he took him on his first duck hunt, the temperature never got above twenty degrees. The decoys were blocks of ice with whiskers (icicles) on their bills. The limit was four ducks each at the time. At eleven o'clock, they lacked one duck having their limit. They decided they'd had enough; it was time to go home and get by some heat. I guess James decided he had given Andy enough indoctrination. Andy's first duck was a drake Mallard.

## The Day It Blew So Hard

The weather report said fifteen to twenty-five southwest, shifting northwest. James was in the Hog Island blind across the Sound near Currituck Club. With a northwest wind, he was in the lee of Hog Island. He said when the wind shifted it came so fast the seas were coming from the southwest and northwest at the same time. His blind was about ninety yards from the marsh.

He called his wife, Elaine, to tell her he was getting ready to take up. He found out she had tried to call him about six times. It was blowing so hard he didn't hear the phone ring.

When he started taking up, he had to run the boat on his knees and the man he had with him had to get on his knees to take the decoys up. The rain was coming down in sheets. By the time he came around Cattle Pen Point, when he went down in the trough of a sea, he couldn't see over either side of it. The whitecaps were thirty-five or forty feet apart.

When they got back to Poplar Branch Landing, they had two rescue squad vehicles, Stanley Griggs with the emergency vehicle, game wardens and the Coast Guard there. He asked one of the Coast Guard boys how hard the wind was blowing, and the guard told him fifty knots. The water was over the bulkhead at the landing. One of the boys standing there at the landing said, "Mr. Guard, we'd see you and then you'd disappear."

Here's how all of this started: Somebody saw a boat turned over and they thought it was his. The word got out to the high school where his son, Jim, was teaching that he better go home; his daddy was having trouble in the sound. Then somebody told Jack, James's brother, they were sorry to hear about James. "What do you mean?" he asked.

"They found his boat turned over and two men are lost." That's how news travels on the Currituck grapevine.

The boat they had seen turned over was a boat that had broken loose from its mooring up the shore in front of Billy Curling's house. There was no one in the boat.

Elaine said the Coast Guard called her about five times wanting to know James's weight, height, etc. She told them he was in the Hog Island blind, but of course that didn't mean anything to them.

James said if he had known it was going to blow that hard he wouldn't have gone hunting. You have to have a lot of respect for that sound. You don't leave in a blow, but sometimes one comes up and you get caught in it and have to deal with it the best you can.

## Men from Raleigh

James said he had been in the sound a lot of rough days. One day, he had two guys from Raleigh. The ice was slush. It looked like big thick hamburger patties—not solid, but thick. They went across the sound to Hog Island. That's three miles. He said the men were undoubtedly the worst shots he'd ever seen in his life. Every few minutes, they'd have ducks come in and they'd miss and miss.

"Mr. Guard, this is fun" they said, to which he replied, "No this is not fun. We should have had both of your limits and my limit and been home an hour ago." About 1:00 p.m., he told them that was it, they were taking up. At the time, he had a sixteen-foot Milford Austin skiff with a spray hood he was using as a gas boat to take the men in. He had a fifteen-foot fiberglass skiff with a six-horsepower outboard motor he was towing his decoys in. After he got his rig up, he started home. When he got to Lone Oak Channel, it was frozen solid, and he couldn't get through. He had to back track and take another route. The line on the skiff was about three inches in diameter with ice. The motor had so much ice on it that it would die out because the air intake would freeze over.

Colon Grandy came out to meet him in the Narrows and asked him if he was alright. He said, "Yeah," and looked up and Colon was gone. He had come out there in the state boat. At the time, Colon was working for Marine Fisheries.

When James got in, his brother was waiting on the dock for him. James's raincoat was a solid sheet of ice. His brother had to help him get out of it. Even his glasses had icicles on them.

## Last Hunt with His Daddy

James and his daddy were tied out in the Narrows. Ice started coming through there and taking their decoys off. James's daddy went and got the gas boat (inboard) and, by the time he got back, ice was piling up on the blind. The decoy skiff was tied to the gas boat and they were picking up the decoys with the gas boat because the ice was taking them away. They were lucky. They got all their decoys.

After they got everything taken up in the Narrows, they went over to the Hog Island blind and tied out there and ended up killing their limit.

When James was a little boy and a bunch of geese would come by, his daddy would pick the last goose in the bunch, shoot him so it would just break his wing and let James shoot him when he hit the water. His daddy was a good enough shot to do that.

James said his daddy never had to buy any shells because the sportsmen gave them to him. A group of hunters usually come down to a lodge together. They would be split up two to a guide. Many times they would get up a pool as to who would kill the most ducks. A lot of times there would be $200 or $300 in the pool. They would want his daddy to shoot because they wanted to win the pool.

## Calling Geese

James said he can't call geese like he used to. He said one time he and his brother were in the Hog Island blind. Bud Lupton had some sportsmen in the next blind over. James and his brother already had their limit of geese. These men heard this honking, but didn't see any geese and wanted to know where the geese were. Bud told them it was those boys. The men didn't believe him so he took them over to the boys blind and got them to honk for them.

Andy, James's son-in-law, made a tape of James calling geese. One day James heard this goose and said, "Where's that goose?" Andy said, "It's you!" He had the tape set up.

## Building a Duck Blind

All of these duck blinds you see in the sound don't just happen. It's a lot of work building a duck blind. Not only is it a lot of hard work, it's expensive by the time you buy 4x4's, 2x6's, plywood for the sides and bottom and 1x4's for slats to hold the bushes or sedge, depending on where the blind is.

Sometimes you are lucky. If we don't have any ice or high tides with strong winds, the blinds may last two or three years with minor repairs. Of course, it has to be bushed every year.

If you are starting from scratch, you have to do as you see James Guard doing in this picture. You sink 4x4's by sharpening the end, then you have a pump with a small gasoline engine and a long hose connected to a piece of pipe, and sometimes you mash the end a little to give it more pressure. If you have a hard bottom, you have to also use a human pile driver like you see James doing in the picture. Then you build the box as you see in the other picture. You put the skiff in front of the blind and sink 4x4's around it. Then you nail 1x4's on each side of them to make a place to hold the bushes. This is called the skiff hide.

James Guard has a good reputation as an agriculture and hunter safety team teacher. He put in a lot of time with his students. He worked hard and expected his students to do the same. If they were not interested, they could get out and do something else.

He loves duck hunting and takes it just as seriously as he did his work. Now, when hunting season is out, he works with his daughter in her landscaping business.

# Fresh Tales from a Native Gunner

*Right*: James Guard being a human pile driver while Andy Blankenship mans the pump to get the pole down. *Courtesy of Andy Blankenship.*

*Below*: James Guard looking at the finished box in one of his blinds. It just needs painting and bushing. *Courtesy of Andy Blankenship.*

# Blanton Saunders

The picture on the opposite page was in my third book, *Currituck: Ducks, Politics, & Outlaw Gunners*. I'm using this picture again because the Saunders family was prominently associated in the early days with duck hunting in Currituck, all the way back to market hunting.

Many years ago, two men from the North Carolina Wildlife Resources Commission interviewed Blanton Saunders. I think that's where they were from, but I haven't been able to find out for sure. Blanton's grandson, Larry Williams, has the tapes and gave me permission to use them in this book.

Blanton's daddy was Elle Saunders, who was a market hunter and guide after market hunting was outlawed.

In addition to guiding, Blanton built skiffs, made shoving poles, and made canvas duck and goose decoys. I also remember when he was deputy sheriff. He had an old four-door Plymouth, and I heard people say that in the floor of the back seat he had a ringbolt, like the kind that goes in the stem post of a boat, that he could handcuff his prisoners to if they were bad. I remember the Plymouth, but I never saw inside of it.

Blanton was a very colorful character. I just wish you could hear the tapes because I can't capture that on paper. I'm going to tell the stories just like he told them and try to spell words as best I can to sound like he said them.

Now for Blanton's stories. They will jump around in no particular order. They came out just like he thought of them.

# Fresh Tales from a Native Gunner

The Saunders family. Sitting in front is Blanton. Bertie and Elle are in the top row. In the middle are Norma, Elsie, Hazel and Ralph. There was one boy, Mervin, who was not in the picture. Ralph was clerk of court for many years. Norma married Ralph Barco. Blanton was a well-known guide in Currituck. He also made decoys, boats and shoving poles and was a deputy sheriff. *Courtesy of the Merrell Family.*

## *Shooting In the Moonlight*

Way back in the market days, I shot 'em in the moonlight, any way you could get 'em, but I didn't do much firelighting because it was harmful to all the boys, and they knew it. You take a light and go firelighting, and yeah, you may get 'em tonight, but you ain't gonna get 'em tomorrow. They ain't gonna stay there. I got records in some of them books there that some of 'em killed over 500 ducks in a day.

## *Watch the Birds*

I've been out there when we were having a good day and we didn't even shoot 'em. We'd just stand there and watch 'em. This fellow Charles Welp from Akron, Ohio, hunted with me thirty-one years and geese came right in the decoys. He said, "Let's not shoot 'em, let's not shoot 'em." He'd stick a camera right through a hole in the bushes and take a picture of 'em and sit there and watch 'em. Same thing with ducks.

# Another Breed of Currituck Duck Hunters

## *Thurmond Chatham*

*These quotes are just like it's on the tape, jumping from one thing to another. Mr. Thurmond Chatham, who owned Dews Island Club, was also a congressman and owned Chatham Blanket Company. He had bought a little dredge and was having some dredging done around the island. Some of the silt was coming down to the Narrows and killing the grass.*

John Poyner, superintendent of Currituck Shooting Club, got holt of it and so forth, so he ask me about it. I says, "Yes, all that silt around Narrows Island when the tides coming in has the water all mucked up thicker than the devil." I says, "Gonna kill the grass." So Mr. Poyner jumped Chatham the first time he saw him about dredging. Says, "If you are going to do your dredging, do it with a north wind so all your silt and stuff will go the other way." That made the old man hot. He wanted to know where did Mr. Poyner get his information. He told him me, and so he wrote me the sassiest letter that you 'bout ever saw. Said to keep my nose out of his business and affairs, so forth and so on. Boy I fired back to him a letter and I never got no reply from that one, I'll tell you that. He's just a man to me; no better than anybody else.

## *Shooting Over Bait*

The Federal Authorities caught Currituck Club shooting over bait many years ago and closed the entire property of Currituck Shooting club for ten days. They couldn't hunt anywhere, baited or not. The members had to go on the outside with the outsiders. I carried some of 'em and they killed more birds than they did in the ponds sometimes.

They'd go in the pond and stay all day long when the limit was twenty-five ducks, and they'd kill maybe seventeen or eighteen, all day long, but they were blasting them and keeping them moving around in the marsh, and they were coming out there to me, and I had a big rig and I was killing the things. When they closed the club, they had to hire the individual guides to take 'em hunting. I carried some of 'em the whole time and we did good.

They said, "Damn, your hunting is better out here than theirs in the ponds." They had a combination: they killed geese on the outside. Very rare they killed geese on the inside, except in some of the big ponds. One time they had thirty ducks and we had fourteen species of ducks...and we had geese too.

Geese used all around me. Rafts of 'em, have for the past two hundred years or more. They were there regular.

*The interviewer asked him if he baited. Currituck Club was baiting and he was getting the benefit.*

Naw, I didn't have to bait. Back when it was lawful, yeah, I baited. I killed more geese over sweet potatoes. Them things crazy over sweet potatoes.

The North Carolina Wildlife Commission was checking the flights of ducks in Currituck. Their weekly report said they had seen twenty-six gadwell. I killed twenty-eight gadwell that same darn week.

Season's through, though...there will be more widgeon killed than any other duck. Now back in the sink box days, canvasback and redheads, they'd go tie right where a raft of them was using. They'd bait 'em up, and there'd be two to seven thousand in a bunch. They'd go put that sink box right in there with two or three hundred decoys. As I told you yesterday, I've seen my daddy and granddaddy shootin' that ten and eight gauge and [they'd] get the barrel so hot, they'd have to stick the barrel overboard. The steam would fly out, and *powyow, powyow,* ready to go again. Shot forty or fifty shells as fast as you could load and shoot.

*The interviewer asked why did he stay around when so many fellows left and went to Norfolk to work.*

Well, I liked it. They maybe made more money than I did, but it weren't the life I wanted. In these books here, in some of 'em, [they] will tell you when I started making decoys and messing with boats with my daddy and granddaddy. It's several pages in several of these books here. It's just somethin' I like to do and put my whole heart in it. I enjoy my life. There's a lot of other boys that wouldn't go out there to shoot a duck. I know several people in the county that never killed a duck, a deer or a bear in their life. They just don't know what life's like. I got a son that wouldn't walk across the road to shoot the biggest bear that ever was—deer or nuthin' else, but duck huntin' he's ready to go. And grandson, he's crazy 'bout it. They'd get up 'fore day and stay up all night to get chance to go duck hunting.

# Another Breed of Currituck Duck Hunters

## *Knowledge Passed On*

*Does it concern you that a lot of the knowledge and skills you have are not going to be passed on?*

Yeah, it really does. I've tried to get Dailey (Williams) interested in coming over here and making boats. If there's anything to be done to his boat he brings it over here and I do it. He's not interested in it. He don't know how to set up a boat. There ain't many around here know how to put a centerboard in a boat so you can sail head into the wind. There was five that used to make shoving poles. Two of them is dead, and Tilman Merrell is quit. He won't even make any for his own boys, or for his brothers or nobody. They all come here to me.

Billy Beasley up here to Coinjock makes some, and damn boy, he can rough 'em up. He can rough up a boat, and he can rough up shoving oars too. I got an order for fifty whenever I can get to 'em. I got a guy in Florida that, whenever I can get ten made, I bundle 'em up and send 'em to him and he sends me a check for 'em, but I ain't gonna be here another century to do this dag stuff, and somebody's gonna do without or patch stuff up.

*You never looked at all that stuff as work, did you?*

No, I enjoy it. As I told you out in the shop yesterday, so many times when my health was good and what not, when I was not taking fishing or duck hunting parties, I was in the shop doin' somethin'— making decoys or oars, and she'd holler for me to come get somethin' to eat. I was busy with paint or fiberglass mixed up and couldn't come eat right then. Don't bother me to miss a meal. I can eat every hour of the clock around. If I was fifteen minutes late, she'd say, "I'm gonna' put your damn bed in the shop. I can't get you in here." Many a time she told me that.

## *Money Made in Market Hunting*

*How about the money made in market hunting?*

I didn't get in on too much of the market hunting. I was a little fellow in the market days, but my daddy and granddaddy made more money out of the sound than they did farming seventy-five or eighty acres of land. There was just a very few of them that market hunted. There was a lot of 'em that if they didn't make it on the farm. Hell with it, they'd make it the next year. They'd get by. They had their own hogs, cows, chickens, eggs and what not.

# Fresh Tales from a Native Gunner

*What did the guides get paid?*

When those clubs first started operating, the guides got $7 a day, and they furnished everything. Then it kept going up. When I first started working at Currituck Club, we got $20 a day and room and board and they furnished all the gas. We furnished our own boats. Transportation to the ponds and back was our problem. They had gas over there by the barrels. You could stay over there or you could go and come.

When you went in the pond days and got your limit of ducks and came in, hung the ducks up and cleaned the man's gun, you were done. If you got in at nine o'clock or stayed all day long. You could come home nights if you wanted to and be back the next morning for breakfast. They never did rush to get out early.

*Author's note: Getting $7 a day may have been true in the 1920s. A lot of these clubs were started in the 1800s. I don't know what guides were paid then.*

## Hunting at the Clubs

*When did you start hunting at the clubs?*
Twenties.
*How many years did you guide for them?*
Well, off and on, for ten or twelve years. Different members would come.
*In other words they would come to you?*
Yeah.
*You weren't really working for the club. You were working for the member?*
Yeah, one of them bought a share in the club. He came down here, he told me, one time. He said, "Tomorrow I want you to go to the clubhouse at nine o'clock and get a telegram." He was playing the stock market heavy. He says, "They'll wire the stock market report to the clubhouse tomorrow." I'd go in and get the telegram and bring it back to him. He'd look at it and smile a grin from ear to ear. Might do that two or three days, then I'd bring him a telegram, and good God Almighty if some of the damn ducks had flew into him and knocked him overboard, he wouldn't have looked no worse.

He told me when he left here one year, he says, "I got enough money and stocks and bonds to live on the rest of my life and all of my present to date born generation if they'll know how to take care of it."

The next September he sent me a telegram that he'd be here the second week of the season if he could borrow enough money to get here. A millionaire today and a pauper tomorrow.

*After the stock market crash, did the hunters stop coming down here?*

No, no, no. I'd say 80 percent of them it didn't make no difference to. The shares in Currituck Club were at one time $10,000 a share. The only way they could buy a share was for a shareholder to pass away or get too old to come down and sell his share, or just want to get out. Then they had a yearly expense to pay the superintendent, marsh guards, cook, county taxes and so forth. This was divided among the shareholders and would run from five thousand to seven thousand, eight hundred a year. It didn't make no difference to them. They'd come on. Hell, they had money.

Pretty good guys. Now there was one guy named Lawrence B. Van Ingen. He passed away several years ago. He was the richest man in the entire club at the time. He told the members at a meeting one day if any of the members wanted to sell their share because of the way he carried on there, he'd buy them out. He liked to get out and drink liquor. He liked to come ashore after he shot his ducks and go to Norfolk.

He fell overboard one day helping me pull the boat over the dike into the pond. I carried him ashore to get dry clothes on, and he gave me a $50 tip. He got several drinks in him then he decided he wanted to go back and shoot some more ducks.

*What did they do with all the ducks they killed?*

Most every day, they shipped them back to New York and had them stored there. When they got home they'd go to some big hotel, invite their friends and have a party, drink liquor, eat duck and carry on.

*What about lay days?*

In Dare County, they could shoot six days. Monday and Tuesday and Thursday and Friday we could shoot. Wednesday and Saturday were lay days, and of course, you couldn't shoot on Sunday, but we had a ninety-day season.

## Bear Hunting

*When did you get time to go bear hunting?*

Oh, when there weren't no duck hunting or fishing going on. Along in the fall of the year, bears were coming in the field. I've shot 'em in the field toting out corn, standing up just like a man with his arms full. He'll go right over the top of a wire fence with an arm full and pile it up in the woods. I could go show you if you were down here two or three weeks from now, piles of corn cobs and shucks that would fill a pick-up truck in a pile thirty to fifty feet from the field where they toted it out.

One night I shot one that had twelve ears of corn in his arm, and I didn't know if he was back to me or belly to me. It was moonlight, and there came up a little scud up over the moon. Charlie Crain down the road here wanted to go with me that night. He's dead now. He said, "I want to hold the flashlight for you." I said, "I don't need no flashlight, Charlie." "Oh," he said, "yeah, give me a five cell flashlight."

Sometimes I have hid up trees. Make a ladder up a tree and climb up the tree at a place where they are coming regular in and out and shoot the son-of-a-bitch out of the tree, and he won't smell you. You got to stay to the lee of one. If he smells you he don't have to see you.

I've been within eight feet of one. It was blowing hard, and I came up on the lee side of him. He had a hog down and I could hear the hog squealing. I'd hear the hog squealing and I'd run through the woods. Then he'd stop squealing. The bear was licking his blood. Then he'd start squealing and I'd run some more until I got to him, but stay on the lee side of him. If he smells you, he's gone and you'll never get him.

He could see me at forty yards in the woods but didn't believe his eyes. I had the gun right on him, and I was just creeping. I said "you make a break and you've made your last one...I'm gonna see how close I can get to you." They don't believe their eyes. They believe their nose. I walked right up to within eight steps of him with him looking right at me.

Back to the corn field. But I shot this one in the corn field that night, and Charlie Crain was standing right back of me. He touched me and said, "shoot him, shoot him," and I didn't know if he was back to me or belly to me. He was about ten rows of corn from me. I know I could hear Charlie's heart beating, but I wanted to be damn sure I was close enough to him. I knowed the wind was blowing a good breeze and he couldn't smell me.

I killed him, and he had twelve ears of corn when he fell down. I've been in the field and never have I seen where they dropped a single ear of corn. I've found piles where they'd have three or four hundred ears. A sow bear with cubs won't let the cubs in the field. They'll stay in the edge of the woods. She'll tote it out to them, and they'll eat it."

*Have you ever chased bear with dogs?*

Yes sir, that I have, and I've killed a many a one and I've lost many a damn dog. Boys cripple 'em, then it's look out.

My wife said I was crazy, and I guess I am to spend so much money on hunting dogs, boats, lumber, decoys, equipment I really didn't need it all. But I get a [kick] out of hunting, and if I could find a good bear dog, and I wanted him, I bought him. It's my money. I worked for it. She didn't go hungry. If she wanted a dress, she bought it.

I've had as many as eight dogs that wouldn't run another thing but a bear. They wouldn't run a fox. They wouldn't run a deer. I wanted bear hunting dogs, and you can't have a dog that'll run everything in the woods and go bear hunting.

From the first of September one year until the deer hunting season opened, I went bear hunting nineteen days and killed or caught twenty-one bear. We caught a lot of the cubs and gave them to the boys, and they took them to the Smokies and turned them loose to get 'em out of the area.

They'd kill everything. Nobody could have hogs out in the woods back then. [The bears] kill cattle, calves, [and] they'd kill deer.

Joe Riggs over here in Camden County had about 125 head of cattle he kept out in the woods. In the fall of the year, he'd pen 'em up and sell the calves and keep the old ones. At one time he was averaging two to three cows or calves a week the bears was killing. Not all bears will kill cattle. The ones with white spots on their chest will. Nearly every one that we killed had a white spot on his chest.

I killed one that had three white spots on his chest. He had been on top of an old cow and chewed her neck until he got her down. Joe heard the cattle raising the devil and he knowed there was a bear in there. He went over in there. The bear smelled him, and he took off.

He came over here to see me, if I'd take the dogs and go over there. I said, "Yeah, I'll go over there in the morning, Joe." He says, "I don't know that the old cow will get up." I says, "Well, it's gonna be hard for them dogs to take the scent of that bear when all the cattle is out there. You know it makes a difference with a dog when he's in the woods by himself with the bear. Hogs will mess up a bear's scent, but once he jumps him, that's it.

They'll run him up a tree. Bay him on the ground and you sneak up there and kill him."

I went out there, and it was two and a half hours before them dogs could even trail because cattle had walked every trail, but they got the trail and we got him. He had three white spots on his chest, and I'd say he weighed 340 pounds. That much weight on top of a cow, and you could see her tracks where she'd been under branches and knocked him off and what not, but he'd get right back on to her.

They eat a gorge out of a fresh kill. Another bear will smell it and come around and eat some until it's two days old. They won't touch it after that. Then its buzzard feed.

They'll go kill another one. Three or four days later he'll go get another calf.

*You ever have one cripple and mess your dogs up?*

Yessiree. I'm telling you I've been in to them dogs when I'd have a bear broke down. Somebody shot him and broke his back or legs. If they don't rush in there and give him the second shot, we never play around with one. Shoot him twice up a tree or what not. Then you don't get your dogs killed up. I've been in there and couldn't shoot the damn thing. Take my knees and push the dogs out of the way. The dogs would cover him up. I'd put a gun right to the side of his head or right In his belly and pull the trigger. Just six inches away. Then sometimes, dogs would be cut or killed.

*What kind of gun do you use?*

Shotgun with buckshot mostly. I've got a big rifle here I kill a few of 'em up a tree with, but mostly shotgun.

"*Where do most of the bears come from?*

Most of 'em merge out of the Dismal Swamp down in this area. There's some in here now. I know where there's several bear. In a few weeks, they'll be in the corn fields when the roast nears get a little bigger.

*Have you ever heard anything about Panthers here in this area?*

Yeah, but none to speak of. The Dismal Swamp might have a very scattered few. Now we got plenty of wild cats in this area.

Now this Edward Temple, a boy from over in Camden, has hunted a lot with me. I'd call Edward and he kept anywhere from twelve to twenty of the bear dogs. That's all he done. He didn't do no duck hunting and what not. Whenever there was a bear come in here and we went after him, 90 percent of the time he was a dead bear. Them dogs would stay by him two days and nights if the wind breezed up, and they lost him or he went up a tree. I had some full blood Airedales that I gave $60 apiece for when they were nine months old. I trained them up with the old dogs that knew what they were doing. I have had bears that the boys couldn't shoot because the dogs were all around him. It'd get so hot for him, he'd go up the tree and he'd drag the dad gum dog eight or ten feet up the tree before the dog would turn loose and fall out. Then the bear would go on up the tree and turn around and look down at them.

I should have had a movie camera with me in a lot of my experiences. That bear slapped that tree so much, he was so mad smacking his mouth, he pulled the bark right off the tree. He wanted to get aholt of 'em, but there was just too many.

One time, Edward Temple's dogs and mine caught a bear in the woods and killed him. He weighed 145 pounds. They stretched him out. I'm telling you by the time we got to him, he just made a few more gasps and that was it. He didn't want to climb. He wanted to stay and fight it out and he lost.

That's when you get a lot of inexperienced dogs killed. I used to have three dogs that knowed what they were doing. They knowed how close to get to him and when to back away. Occasionally in the thick brush, one would get killed. I've toted 'em out and carried 'em to the vet and got 'em sewed up. A damn dog that I paid $100 or $125 for and tears run right out my eyes. He just made a mistake. He got too close.

### *Back to duck hunting now*

Back in 1928–1930, I killed over 400 Canada geese a season and 900 and some odd ducks.

*How many geese did you kill back in the 1960s?*

I think the limit then was down to four maybe, and twelve or fifteen ducks or somethin' like that, but I've killed my share of 'em boys if I never kill another one.

*What makes a good guide?*

Like to do it (laughs); gotta instinct to love to do it. The most of the boys that really are on the ball started young. That grandson of mine, I carried him in the sound when he was eight years old. Dailey, my son, I carried him out there when he was a little fellow. Hell, when he was twelve years old, I

# Fresh Tales from a Native Gunner

turned him loose with a boat with a fishing party in the summertime. When he was fourteen years old, I turned him loose with a shotgun. On holidays and Saturdays, he was in the sound.

*You say he was guiding fishing parties at twelve years old?*

Yes sir (laughs), but he don't care much about it now. Then he wanted some money. I had the boat here and the equipment and he'd carry 'em.

Sometimes, he wouldn't judge them squalls coming up. A time or two, he like to of sunk a boat and that kinda brought him 'round. You know I can watch these decoys here and the signs, etcetera, like my daddy and granddaddy. They didn't have any barometer or what not, and they could tell when it was going to blow like the devil next day or what not. Watch these sun dogs they call them, sky and what not. They could tell when there was coming a rain or snow.

I've been out there some bad times. One storm we had, they recorded sixty mile per hour winds at Cape Henry, and I made it in. That particular night I made five round trips across the sound bringing in ones that were stranded and couldn't make it.

Willie Barnard started in. He sunk his boat. They all went ashore in the marsh, he was close to the marsh. I finished getting them all in by two o'clock in the morning. It was cold wintertime.

The boys couldn't make it across the Sound. I said, "If you'll stay put, stay to this guard camp, I'll come get all of you. I'm not going to overload on one trip, because I know what to expect," and they stayed put. I was nearly all night long hauling them in, but I brought them in.

*How could you get them in?*

Well I had a bigger boat and I had plenty of power, and I had the guts to tackle it (laughs). That was the main thing. The wind was blowing the top off the waves.

One day I had a guy from Consolidated Aircraft that was hunting with me when it was blowing forty miles per hour. He saw that I knew how to operate the damn boat. We went across the sound and didn't take a quart of water in the boat.

## Boat Building

*Author's note: Blanton built a boat for the North Carolina Wildlife Resources Commission for Game Warden Howard Forbes Jr. to use. Herbert must have been a game warden in the Pamlico Sound area at the time.*

*How was your boat different from other boats?*

Well, I been out there and seen the boats that swamped that weren't made right to take it (laughs). And I knew that changes could be made in 'em. The widths and what not and the cut up in the bow.

When Dailey first got his, she wanted to lope a little, but we finally solved that problem. It's more than just grabbing a bunch of boards and nailing them together.

Now Herbert, he's in rougher water than the other boys are. He's got a lot of rough water down there. I built him a boat I thought would take it. I don't think he's been scared in her too many times.

This boat was built for the North Carolina Wildlife Resources Commission by Blanton Saunders to be used by Howard Forbes Jr., game warden. When Howard Jr. retired, they gave him the boat. Years later he gave it to The Whalehead Preservation Trust. Wilson Snowden and Travis Morris hired Jimmy Markert to restore it for the Whalehead Trust. *Author's collection.*

# Fresh Tales from a Native Gunner

There is a lot of boys that have built boats that, with a following sea when it's rough, would stick her nose right down and go on right out of sight in the next sea. You can make her so her nose will come up.

*Your boats up here all got to be flat bottom because of the shallow water don't they?*

Yeah, yeah, the bigger part of them are.

*You can't have a boat with a V bottom can you?*

Yeah, yeah, V bottom. Tunnels so they'll run in shallow water.

I got a map here that shows the water depth all over Currituck Sound. There's some channels that's got thirty feet of water. There's one place I know that I can wade from the shore on this side to the beach. That's 3.5 miles, and I can wade it other than two places of 120 yards. I would have to swim the channel that is over my head, but the rest of it is shallow.

In the Little Narrows right at the Devil's Elbow, the water is thirty two feet deep. The current keeps it cut out.

## *Lived Anywhere Else? And What Happened to the Ducks?*

*Do you think you could have lived anywhere but the Currituck area?*

(Laughs)Yeah, where they had good duck hunting, and they had bear and deer hunting.

You can go up into Maine, and some places you can shoot black duck, and a few scattered other ducks, but according to the sports writers that have been in here in years gone by, this is the best combination hunting there is anywhere in the country, and they have hunted from the Arctic Circle to South America.

*What's happened to the ducks now?*

They've changed farming practices up in Maryland. Where they used to raise vegetables they are raising grain now, and the ducks and geese have no reason to come on down farther, and it don't freeze out enough but what they can get water and plenty of food.

The widgeon usually come in before the season opens and [is] gone by the time the season's in. We used to open the season by the first day of November.

I well remember several years I was the first one in to the dock on opening day of the season. The limit was eight geese and twenty-five ducks. I was in to the dock that morning at 11:15 with sixteen geese and fifty ducks.

Graft Beasley went up to the store and got some more shells. The two of us went back and we killed sixteen more geese and forty-one ducks that evening on opening day, the first day of November. That's more than a lot of 'em kill in the whole damn season now.

*Is it better for the season to open in December or November?*

We kill more duck, Terry, with it opening in November. You get these widgeon and so forth, and they were the main duck. You don't get canvasback and redheads early, but you haven't been able to shoot 'em for years. Even back in the market days, you never got many canvasback and redheads until December and January. The marsh ducks, they come early.

## Caught in the Ice

The trouble with the late season is the freeze ups. One freeze up cost me over $1,000. That time I got out there in the boat, and the ice cut her down. Got on a shoal, and the wind was blowing hard. I was trying to save some of the skiffs out in other blinds, messing around trying to get 'em bunched up and get to the guard camp. The wind breezed up, and the ice started moving and it got me.

*What do you mean cut her down?*

Cut the side right out of her. Jammed on a shoal and that ice coming right by cutting it just like a pair of scissors. Cut the damn side right out of her. I got pictures right here.

I got the same boat right here sittin' in the shop. I went and got it and took a pattern of the good side and put it back in her and used it twenty more years. It's a big inboard job. I hadn't used it in ten or twelve years. I went to outboards and smaller boats. You could get on out there in the sound quicker, and you could get ashore in the evening quicker. We shot until four twenty.

## The Compass and Going With Game Wardens

I keep checking myself year in and year out by the daylight, checking my points and see how the compass and so forth position. I can put the compass in the boats and set 'em and get my watch out and know how many minutes to run that course at a certain rate of speed.

# Fresh Tales from a Native Gunner

A lot of 'em don't get a compass out until they need it, and then they don't know what to do with it. Don't know the courses or how to run or what not. That boat parked over there in the shade? It's got three compasses in it. We might run a whole season and never need a compass. Then again, there might be six to ten mornings or nights in a season we need one.

That day that Rupert West and Bruce Etheridge went with me, the number of the blind we were going to was 255. We got up to it, and Mr. Etheridge said, "Whose blind is this?"

Rupert says, "This is the one we're gonna shoot in."

Mr. Etheridge says, "I can't believe it. I ain't seen a damn thing since we left the dock. I went by all the other blinds and through the marsh, and it's crooked through there.'

*Didn't you go out with the game wardens some?*

Yeah, I been with Howard Jr. and Scott, (local State Game Wardens) when they had that old big boat, house boat. They'd call them if boys got stranded. If I'd go with 'em to take the controls they'd go, while it was snowing and what not. I've been out with the boys and retrieved a lot of 'em.

*You've been out looking for game wardens too, haven't you?*

"Yeah, a time or two I been out there to get 'em.

*Anybody ever die out there you know of?*

Yeah, we've had several. A few had heart attacks.

*You ever have anybody freeze to death?*

No, but we've had a lot of 'em drown, and a lot of 'em killed in shooting accidents.

I've been out there with dynamite and raised bodies. I've been out there with a long net and raised bodies. Caught 'em in the nets. Fished 'em up. In general as much hunting as is going on, the accident rate is very, very small. I'm cautious, and the rest of the boys are too now.

*Author's note: Rupert West was from Moyock, North Carolina. He wrote a lot of articles about hunting and fishing for leading national sports magazines. The last twelve years of his life, he worked for the Department of Conservation and Development. He died in 1946.*

*R. Bruce Etheridge was from Manteo, North Carolina. He was Director of the Department of Conservation and Development from 1933 until 1949.*

## Mad Hunters

I've had some of the hunters get mad with me. It don't matter a damn to me. When he gets to drinking so much, I'm gonna take that gun away from him. He ain't gonna fling that thing all around my head. I might get killed the next day, I go hunting in five minutes, but I've managed to get by. I've had some shots go by close to my head and younguns' fooling with the damn gun and she'd go off and shoot a hole through the blind. One guy shot right between my legs one time. I took the gun away from him. The damn fool loaded it drunk. He had too much to drink.

I don't object to 'em taking a drink of whiskey, but when they get a little bit too much, I'm gonna take that gun away from him.

There's a doctor up the state that I hit over the head with a damn gun. He tied into me going to take that gun away from me. I said "Now listen, I told you you'll get this gun when you get ashore. You can put it in your car."

He says "No, that gun belongs to me. I've paid for it, I'm going to load it and shoot some more."

I said "No you ain't." He tied into me, and I hit him over the head and knocked his ass down in the blind with the barrels of the thing. I meant that he wasn't gonna have it anymore.

## Stay With the Sportsmen

*Do you stay with the sportsmen all day?*

Yeah. We stay with 'em. A lot of places they'll take you to the blind and drop you off and come back later and pick you up. Here, the guide stays with 'em and retrieves the ducks.

Some of 'em, that Ray Trellinger sports writer, wore waist waders, and he got a lot of kick out of retrieving his own ducks. Every one of my blinds is on sandy bottom, near just like walking out there in the yard. Now some of the boys got muddy bottom. You can't wade. You just go right on down.

*How do you take up the decoys when the wind's blowing?*

Now, with a little outboard motor, we go up wind, cut her off and drift through 'em and pick 'em up. Crank her up and do the same thing again until you get 'em all up.

# Fresh Tales from a Native Gunner

Before, we had little outboard motors, we had to pole up wind, throw an anchor, keep letting the line out and pole from side to side and rake 'em in with an oar until you got 'em all in.

*How long will it take you to take up?*

Well, with the motor, it'll take fifteen to eighteen minutes.

*How many decoys?*

Sixty to seventy-five. I ain't got them little rigs. Laughs. I got eighty or ninety ducks and twenty or twenty-five geese. Now I've got thirty-five floating snow geese and a hundred and sixteen silhouettes that I stick in the marsh and stick 'em every damn way. I kill the birds. Son, if you got the equipment, you can kill 'em.

Lot of 'em up there with small rigs. They kill a few ducks. If you are going to do anything, do it right.

## *Money Making?*

*Do you make any money caring hunters?*

Yeah, I make cigarette money.

*How much money would your granddaddy make?*

Ah, they'd make maybe $600, $800, maybe $1,000 clear of expenses and what not. That's more than they'd make on the damn farm.

*How much do you make, clear of all your expenses?*

Well, one year I had a lot of breakdowns and tore up my motor and what not hitting duck blinds the ice had scattered, and I couldn't see. In one day, I tore up a fifty horsepower Mercury motor that cost me $645 to fix. In an average season, you'll hit $1,500–$1,800.

## *Stern Lesson*

Dailey, my boy, ran into a duck blind the ice had cut off. Stobs and stuff was left, and he didn't see it. He was coming over there and running a right good rate of speed, and tore part of the damn stern out of the boat. [The] motor jumped off it overboard, running on the bottom. The cables and controls and stuff was what held it, so he could pull it in and pole it in here.

## *Blind License*

*Are there a lot of blinds cut down out there?*

Yessir, and they are dangerous. Way back, the license on a blind was a quarter. Then they went to a dollar. Now they are $8.50 for an outside bush blind. Marsh point blinds are $10.50. When they raised that fee, the state gets two dollars for every blind license in Currituck Sound. Then there was supposed to be two dollars per blind to clean up all the duck blinds and things that people would hit out there. It's supposed to be thousands of dollars in that pot. In Currituck Sound there are six hundred and twenty six licensed blinds. There are eight hundred and forty marsh blinds.

The blinds in the ponds the ice don't cut down. It don't have the pressure, the chance to move. The outside blinds, the more open water there is, it cuts them off. There's blinds out there now that are cut off even with the water. Stobs are just under the water. Guy come by and hit one of them, and he'll tear up a damn propeller or motor, and when it's rough bouncing up and down, they punch a hole in 'em.

I patched a boat last year the first part of the season. A guy run into a stob and punched a hole in the side of the damn thing. He got everybody on one side to hold that side up and made it in to the dock. He put it on a trailer and brought it up here to me and I patched the damn thing that night for him.

## LEAVING TIME

A lot of folks have fussed with me about leaving. The federal law says you can shoot thirty minutes before sunrise and shoot until sunset. The guides don't want it, so the county board set a regulation you couldn't leave the dock until thirty minutes before sunrise and had to take up at 4:20. That gave them all time to get in. Some of those bad days and all, it's the best thing. It's a county law, but it's enforced by the State Game Wardens.

# Fresh Tales from a Native Gunner

## *Waterfowl Population and Float Blinds*

*How is the waterfowl population now?*
It's low, but it's come back up some. It's crept up the ladder from what it was a few years ago. There's more hunting pressure on 'em. Where there used to be a thousand hunters hunting in Currituck Sound, there's twelve hundred and fifty now.

*How has the outboard motor affected waterfowl?*
Oh, not too good to a certain extent. There's a lot of the boys that'll go out tie out in the blinds and if there's a raft of ducks nearby they'll go run 'em up. They're gonna congregate out there in a raft. If there's not much doing he's gonna go with that damn outboard motor and run 'em up again. If they light down over yonder some other guy'll run 'em up over there. Well, it ain't long before I've seen them go out in the ocean where they can get some rest...

Now these float blind boys. They'd see a raft of ducks here and he'd go around and run 'em up and maybe get a few shots. They'd go a mile or two down, and he'd go get 'em up again. Well. Where they gonna go? The boys ha[ve] slowed up right much on that chasing deal. There's a few of 'em even now, one bunch of geese come light in front of 'em. Ain't long before he's got 'em up. Let 'em go and come on their own and it's good hunting.

## *Blue Peters and Firelighting*

*Anybody shoot blue peters out of the boat now?*
No, I never told you about that. We used to ring shoot 'em.

Ain't never any of the books ever wrote up much about ring shooting blue peters. Four or five boats get together out where there's from one to five thousand blue peters and stay close together. Sea gulls and eagles used to keep 'em bunched up. Get around 'em a gunshot apart, then somebody go in there and start flying them things out. They'd kill a 150 to 200. Give everybody in the neighborhood blue peters.

They eat the same feed other ducks eat. Now a lot of places they claim they are musty and they can't eat 'em. You have to skin 'em instead of pick 'em.

*Have you ever done much firelighting here?*

Never done too much firelighting here. Your daddy and your granddaddy and Seth Garrington had really done as much of it as anybody.

Old fellow I knew would take a boat and shove up to 'em and never touch the side of the boat with the oar. Sneak up on to 'em. They never knew a thing until he shot. He could shove that damn boat and never touch anything. Daddy could. Only thing they could hear was the oar sliding through the water. You bump the side of the boat trying to get up to them, and they're gone. As long as that light's on and they don't hear nothin'. They'll sit right there and swim together.

I haven't been able to find out who interviewed Blanton, and he was the only one I could hardly hear on the tapes. As I said in the beginning, I knew Blanton Saunders, and after hearing these tapes, I felt like they were too good not to be passed on to future generations.

I never heard of shooting blue peters the way Blanton was talking about with four or five boats. The way we did it around Maple was in Coinjock Bay, where there weren't many houses nearby. Bells Island was not developed then, and around the rest of the bay was marsh. No houses.

We'd take a gas boat and keep circling a bunch of blue peters until they got in a tight knot, then we'd go up wind of them, open the throttle wide open, and come down through 'em and shoot three times and pick up forty or fifty. There must have been ten thousand in Coinjock Bay. You couldn't do this at Waterlily unless it was foggy. Too many folks watching you.

# Hunting With an Eighty-Two-Year-Old Woman

Barbara Brumsey Smith and I are both Currituck natives. We grew up together and ran around together. Not as boyfriend and girlfriend, but she was like one of the boys. Her daddy was a farmer. In 1948, snap beans sold real good and her daddy, Mr. Carl Brumsey, bought her a new blue two-door torpedo Roadmaster Buick. She was the only one in our crowd who had their own car. She'd pick up a load of us and we'd go to Elizabeth City to the movies or just ride around.

Barbara and I have duck hunted together since we were kids. I'm not going into that because I told about it in my second book, *Currituck Memories and Adventures: More Tales from a Native Gunner*.

Barbara has her own duck blind right in front of her house in Currituck. She and I are both so old it's not safe for us to go hunting together alone, because if one of us fell overboard, the other one of us couldn't pull the one that fell over in.

My son-in-law, West Ambrose, has been mighty good to Barbara. He builds and bushes her blind every year and takes her hunting. I asked him to write a story about taking an old woman hunting and here it is in his own words.

Barbara Glenn Brumsey Smith on her dock standing beside her boat with one redhead and two blackheads. *Courtesy of West Ambrose.*

## Hunting with Barbara

It's a cold gray day on the Sound, another poor day of duck hunting. At 6:30 in the evening, I was glad to look forward to a warm home and supper, thanks to a good woman, my wife. As I walked into the house, she said,

"Supper is ready." I smiled and thanked the Lord for good things.

"How was duck hunting?"

"It's kinda poor, real poor." At the time, the season closed the Saturday after Thanksgiving and opened back up on December 10, and went until January 15. We could only kill three ducks per gunner per day, and you would be lucky to kill a duck.

To say the least, it was poor, and most men had quit except for the die hards. I was one. I believed then, as I believe now, the Federal Government was trying to stop duck hunting on Currituck Sound while other states had more liberal duck hunting. It did not work.

From my encounter with duck hunters, they are not quite right. Why crawl out of bed at 4:00 a.m. to run across the sound in an open boat, make a tie and gun ducks? Like I stated, not quite right. It gets in your blood and there is nothing you can do about it. Not exactly normal, but why be normal if it's dull?

# Fresh Tales from a Native Gunner

As we ate supper, Ruth (my wife) said, "Barbara Glen called and wants you to go gun ducks with her."

"Who is Barbara Glen and why do I want to go duck hunting with a woman, and how old is she?" I asked. Ruth told me she was a friend of her family and that Barbara Glen wanted me to go. "I ain't taking no old woman duck hunting," I said.

"Her phone number is on the counter," Ruth told me. "Call her." I could tell my wife's mind was made up. It was time to run up the white flag. The battle was over.

I called Barbara Glen and received a warm, but blunt, response. "Be at my house at 6:00 in the morning," she told me, then gave me directions on how to get there. Well, I figured I'd humor the old woman, wind the day up and never go back.

On Saturday, I arrived at her home, pulled into the driveway, got out of my old truck and there she was, dressed in coveralls and hollering, "Over here!" I put on my fowl weather gear, shotgun and shell box in hand. As I walked, the wind was blowing north/northeast at about ten to fifteen miles per hour, and the tide was down. I had wind but not much water, which suited me just fine. About that time, I saw a green boat with a motor sitting on the shore and thought, "What the hell is this?" She came up and greeted me, and we talked a few minutes. My first impression was, "I like the old gal." I asked her about the boat and she told me to shove it down the ramp and start it and let's go.

Well, I did. Meanwhile, she stood on the shore waiting for the motor to crank. I pulled and pulled on that motor and it would not crank. Barbara Glen hollered, "What's wrong?"

I said, "The damn thing won't crank." So I poled the boat back to shore. She said, "Are you getting fuel in the line?" "Yes," I told her, "everything looked fine." Then I pulled the vent cap off the four gallon gas can and told her it was full of water and frozen up. The next thing I know, she went on a cussing spree. Not bad cussing, about normal. I've heard worse and said worse.

"They told me there was fresh gas in that tank." ("They" being her husband, Millard, a good man who is now deceased; and her son, Randy.)

"I am treated like a Queen, like a QUEEN around here." She was pissed off big time, and "treated like a Queen" ain't what she meant. Well, she looked at me and asked, "What do we do now?" I told her I had a six-horse motor and six gallons of good fuel at my shop and it would only take twenty minutes to go there and back. Her eyes lit up. "Hurry up and get back!" Well, I hauled ass as fast as I could and arrived back at her house, took the hunk of junk motor off her boat and put the frozen gas can off to one side. Then I slammed my motor on the stern, attached the hose from the tank to the motor, shoved the boat overboard, fired it up, picked her up at the dock and made for the blind.

By this time, it was eight o'clock. Enough time had been wasted. I figured we would tie out, sit in the blind until noon, not shoot any ducks and call it a day.

Well, that ain't exactly what happened. As we tied out, I eyeballed her decoys. They looked poor and were stacked half-assed. "This ain't good," I thought. After tying out, I put the boat in the skiff hide and helped her in the blind.

We loaded up and sat ready to shoot. "This is one half-assed operation," I figured. Then we started to talk about where are you from? Who do you know? What brought you to Currituck? In general, small talk.

Well, I glanced off to one side and, damn, a "boobie" had swam into the decoys. A "boobie" is a Rudy Duck, or some call 'em Dollar Ducks. When market hunting, they got a dollar apiece for "boobies."

She said, "Shoot him." I said, "Hell he's on the swim, Barbara Glen." She told me, "I don't care. I want ducks to eat." So I busted his ass.

Before long, a Black Duck swam in and she shot him. By eleven o'clock, we had killed two boobies and two blackheads. All on the swim. I don't care to shoot swimming ducks but that's how the ducks came and that's how they got shot. She told me that day she liked them on the swim. She could shoot the ducks better that way. Also she didn't want to shoot hens, only drakes because hens reproduced and it only took a few drakes to service the hens. I had to agree.

Well, we wrapped it up and pulled the plug on that day's hunt around noon. I told her I would go with her again.

About a week later, she called the house and wanted to go duck hunting that Wednesday. I told her yes, I'd take off that day. Since I did not trust her motor or fuel, I took my own.

As I shoved the boat down the ramp, poled out and then fired the motor, I thought to myself, "Something ain't exactly right the way those ducks swam into the decoys like that."

# Fresh Tales from a Native Gunner

Once we tied out and got in the blind, I said, "I know you are feeding around this blind. Ducks don't swim in like this for the hell of it." She laughed and said, "I am. I've been doing this for fifty years and don't intend to stop. Anyway, we don't shoot over our limit, our shells and shotguns are legal, and I only hunt this blind twice a week. It ain't like it's a slaughterhouse out here." "Well," I said, "I agree with you on that, but the law has another way of thinking."

Barbara Glen said, "I don't care about the law, we are not slaughtering ducks. I only kill what I can eat."

Well, hell, she had a point and I didn't argue. Sometimes the law ain't exactly right all the time no matter how you slice it. I know. I've had a few run-ins with the law and felt like I got the short end of the stick.

Over time, Barbara Glen could not put the boat in the sound by herself, and she asked me to feed. I told her I would, but I would not feed around the blind anymore because it was "too dicey." She raised hell about it, but I put my foot down and that was that.

Anyway, she talked me into keeping up her blind and feeding as she was getting on and could not do it. I gave her my word and have been doing it for at least twenty years now.

I no longer feed around the blind. I do put it as legal as the clubs do on the sound. What's good for the goose is good for the gander. I believe she gets a kick out of just watching the ducks as she drinks on a toddy bourbon and ginger.

We had a lot of good hunts at that blind and I brought along friends of mine who hunted with us. All had good times and she never minded the friends I took. Barbara Glen gets along with them and came to know and like them all.

I have carried her to many blinds on the sound from Currituck proper to Poplar Branch along with my friends. Good times all the way around. Hell, who could ask for more.

Now things have changed and I take her when she wants to go, not as often as before. I will say at the age of eighty-two, she shoots a duck on the fly while John Thomas and I congratulate her on a good shot. "The old Lioness still has teeth."

What started out as half-assed turned into a genuine friendship better than I could ask for. Barbara Glen would give you the coat off her back, but is tight with a dollar. She will squeeze a nickel so hard it will make the buffalo holler. I dearly love her. She once asked, "What will you do when I'm gone?" I said, "Calm down. Don't ask me that."

She persisted, "What will you do?"

I told her, "I'll burn that blind down. Call it a day. It would not be the same without you." Of course, the people around there would raise hell about it but, to quote Captain Rhett Butler, "Frankly, my dear, I don't give a damn." They will never know what it is like to sit in a blind on a cold raw day with someone you like and share what we shared. My Lord knows and that's all that matters to me. I thank God for my good times on this earth and more to come. Who could ask for better?

# The Intracoastal Waterway Trip of the *Deb Nan*

Have you ever wondered what it would be like to take a trip down the Intracoastal Coastal Waterway from North Carolina to Fort Lauderdale, Florida? If you have, read on and I'll take you on my first trip.

For you to appreciate the story, I have to introduce you to the characters that went on the trip...and I do mean characters.

I had always wanted to make the trip, but never thought I'd get the chance. That all changed with a phone call from Dickie Ferrell. He and his twin brother, Bobby, had sold their sawmill in Moyock, and their fishing pier along with its restaurant, motel and twenty some cottages in Rodanthe. They were going to retire.

They still had a forty-eight foot Tiffany Sportfisherman named *Deb Nan*. It was named after Bobby's daughter, Debbie, and Dickie's daughter, Nancy. After this trip, the name was changed to *Wild Goose* because *Deb Nan* sounded like "dead man" on the VHF radio. I had fished with them on this boat several times out of Hatteras.

Back to Bobby and Dickie. They are twins and are native Currituckers, born and raised in Currituck, North Carolina. Their Daddy, Earl Ferrell, was a logger, and their Mother was a schoolteacher.

Bobby and Dickie both graduated from NC State University with degrees in forestry. They were in the ROTC while at NC State and had to pull a stint in Korea during the Korean Conflict. Dickie killed a pheasant over there with an M-1 rifle and sent him to the general. The general said, "Any man that can kill a pheasant with an M-1 rifle, give him a shotgun and let him kill pheasants for me."

Dickie had a little higher rank than Bobby and could give Bobby orders. That didn't go over too well.

One thing about Bobby and Dickie: they were always fighting. I could write a book just about them. They were several years older than me, but one time when I was in high school, I was riding with them. We were going to a formal dance. Bobby sat on the flower Dickie had for his date. They stopped right down Tull Creek road, got out of the car and fought until one of them got his shirt bloody and we had to go back to their house for him to change his shirt before we could go pick up the girls.

When they got out of the army, they started a saw mill operation called Ferrell Brothers' Mill. They bought three thousand acres of timber land behind the mill. They put in large canals to drain the land, then logged it and took it in as farmland.

Daddy told me one time those boys would buy Currituck County if they could buy it on time. Speaking of that, they bought Bells Island from Mrs. Gray after Mr. Gray died. This was in the late 1960s.

I couldn't write this book without saying how generous they were with what they had. When they owned Bells Island, and the clubhouse was still there, they would let anybody use it for weddings, parties, and other celebrations. The only condition was the people had to clean up the mess before they left. I have been to a party there that had everybody from the workers in the log woods to Andy Griffith. They didn't discriminate.

The next character is Joe Ferrell Jr. He had just retired from the air force. Joe Jr. was older than me, too, but he, Carter Lindsey and W.L. Northern would let me tag along sometimes when I was little around the wharf at Currituck. Joe was always up to some mischief. I remember one moonlit night, we were sailing in Carter's sailboat in Currituck Sound, and Joe climbed the mast and tried to turn the boat over.

Now we had two boys on the trip: Bobby's boy, Robert, and Dickie's boy, Billy. Then there was Captain Jack Hoffler. I will leave the rest about Captain Jack for the end of the story except to say he is a very colorful character and very good natured. I think most of you will be as surprised as I was when I found out more about Captain Jack, which was years after the trip.

# Fresh Tales from a Native Gunner

Joe Ferrell Jr. and Carter Lindsey and Carter's sail boat. *Courtesy of Mary Ellen Snowden Williams.*

I got up about 5:00 a.m. on Saturday, February 13, 1982, and heard the wind howling. I told Frances I was sure we were not going to leave in that weather, but I'd get ready just in case. I was sitting in the chair about half asleep when, fifteen minutes later, a Suburban pulled up with Bobby, Dickie, Robert, Billy and Elaine, who was going to drive the car back from the dock. Robert jumped out to help me get my gear, and as I walked out the door I heard some very hot language coming from the vehicle. "What am I getting myself into?" I thought to myself.

We soon arrived in Elizabeth City without much conversation. When we got out, Robert told me his Daddy and Dickie had already had their fight and he thought everything would be all right. I later found out the fight was about which one was going to sleep in the room with me, and which one was going to sleep in the room with the boys.

Let me say here and now that things were all right. I was on the boat eleven days. That is a long time for seven people to be on a boat without getting on each other's nerves. I have never been with a more congenial group. We really got along fine, including Bobby and Dickie.

We loaded our gear aboard the boat. Captain Jack had the engines and generator running, lights burning and was chomping at the bit to go. Joe Jr. was already aboard, as was Jack's wife and his two daughters. Jack got them ashore and told Elaine he would take good care of us. We got underway at 6:30 a.m. I felt good that we had a competent captain.

The forward stateroom has three bunks, which were occupied by Dickie, Joe Jr. and Billy. Bobby and I slept in the port stateroom, which has an adjoining head. Robert and Captain Jack slept on the sofa, which converts into two single beds for the first two nights, after which it was warm enough for Captain Jack to sleep on the flying bridge and the boys occupied the sofa.

As we got underway, Dickie was on the bridge with Captain Jack. The boys had gone up forward and gone to bed. Joe Jr., Bobby and I were in the main cabin. The old Detroits were humming along at 2,400 rpm. The wind was blowing a gale but was on our stern, so everything was going smooth. After a few minutes, I decided to go up on the bridge. Captain Jack was looking for the old Wade Point light tower, which he soon saw. I thought it was kinda strange for him to be looking for that instead of the number one buoy, which would have been closer. The chart shows the Intracoastal going the way he was going, so I didn't think much about it. I came on back down below. As soon as we got in Albemarle Sound, it got very rough, and water was coming in the windows on one side. Joe Jr. got some towels, and we started mopping water. Soon we felt the boat bump bottom. That surprised me in that an experienced captain had hit the shoal at Alligator River Bar. All we could see from down below was sheets of water on the cabin windows. Now we were having to mop water on the other side of the boat, which means we had changed course. Then we changed sides again. This went on for nearly two hours. Finally, Bobby said, "I'm going up top and see what's going on." He came right back down and called for me to see if I knew where we were.

Captain Jack says he isn't lost," Bobby said, "he just doesn't know where he is." As soon as I got on the bridge, I recognized Croatan Light and the Umstead Bridge, which was in the opposite direction from where we wanted to go. I also saw the middle-ground marker. This was the beginning of my losing faith in our "captain who knew all things." After showing him where we were, I went back below to mop water. About this time, Robert came out and said he had just been thrown out of his bunk. He said he had been in the ocean many times in that boat, but had never been thrown out of his bunk or heard the timbers creak like that.

We passed under Alligator River Bridge at 10:30 a.m. and arrived in Belhaven at 1:45 p.m. We first stopped at River Forest Manor and could find nobody to give us fuel. Then we went to Jordan's, and no one was there. We went to a fish dock and it was the same story. We came back to River Forest

# Fresh Tales from a Native Gunner

Manor and finally got fuel and got underway again at 3:00 p.m. When we got to Goose Creek, just north of Hoboken, we saw many blackheads. It was 5:00 p.m. when we docked at one of the fish houses in Hoboken, where the trawlers tie up. Nobody was around, and we didn't have power, so we ran the generator all night. Captain Jack cooked a good spaghetti supper.

On February 14, we got underway at 6:30 a.m. It was a nice day when we headed out. You are supposed to turn right at Maw Point and head up the Neuse River. I knew that because I had just been there in my boat in October. Captain Jack saw some marker way out in Pamlico Sound he thought we should go to. Dickie and I finally convinced him to make a right turn since we didn't want to go to Ocracoke this trip! We passed by Oriental and headed up Adams Creek. When we got to the turn at the range marker, we ran aground. I assume some responsibility for this since I was looking at the chart too. We were lucky. We managed to back off without damaging anything. We went on past Morehead City and stopped at Spooner's Creek Marina just below Morehead to take on fuel at 10:00 a.m. We departed there at 10:23, and had a nice trip on down to Southport Marina, where we arrived at 4:15 p.m. and took on fuel. This is where we should have stayed. Captain Jack wanted to push on to Little River, South Carolina, so we did. When it got dark, Captain Jack summoned me to the bridge to connect the spot light and read the chart. We made Little River Marina at 7:30 p.m., but nobody was there. We found an electric box and plugged into that. Captain Jack told the boys there was a bar or something in Little River. The boys took off up a muddy road but soon came back having found nothing but a grocery store. I don't remember what we ate for supper that night, but everybody was so tired I think we just ate a sandwich. This was the most miles we made in one day (168).

The next day, we left Little River at 6:40 a.m. and stopped at Bucksport to take on fuel. This is located on the Waccamaw River, which is a very pretty, winding river that reminds me very much of the Pasquotank. We arrived at Charleston Municipal Marina at 3:40 p.m., where we fueled up and tied up for the night. They have nice showers there, which we were all thankful for. The dockmaster told the boys a place to go, so they took off. The rest of us were a little later getting ready, but we finally got a cab. Captain Jack knew a place he said was great. We asked the cab driver about this and he said it was just a tourist trap. He advised us to go to the Old Town Restaurant if we wanted good food at a reasonable price. He took us there, and the food was great. On the way over there, Captain Jack was asking the driver about places that he had been to in 1947. We got tickled at this because it was before the driver was born.

The chickens were so good we decided to take some back with us so the boys could have some the next day. In the process, we went out and unintentionally did not leave a tip. We were standing outside the restaurant waiting for a taxi when the owner, who was Greek, came out and asked me what country we were from. I should have told him Greece, but I laughed and said "America."

"I thought it was customary in America to leave the waitress a tip. She is having a fit in there," he said. Dickie assured him it was unintentional and took care of it.

On February 16, we left Charleston at seven on a rainy morning, and made it to Beaufort, South Carolina, at 11:30 a.m. At 12:20, we anchored in the entrance to Port Royal Sound because of fog. When the fog lifted, we got underway at about 1:43 p.m. When we went by Harbor Town on Hilton Head Island, we were taking pictures and not paying attention to where Captain Jack was going. It turned out he should have made a right turn here, but didn't. The next thing we knew we were engulfed by fog and we could see marker number 3. We looked at the chart, but this was not on the chart we had. At 3:20 p.m., we decided we better anchor. When the engines were shut down, we could hear the surf pounding, so we figured we must be in the inlet. Captain Jack said he wasn't lost, but again just didn't know where he was. We decided we had best rig up a mast light, so we ran a drop cord up one of the outriggers. We heard a tugboat talking in the ocean, so Captain Jack got him on the radio and the tug captain said he saw us on his radar and that we were just inside the inlet.

Just before midnight, the fog lifted and you could see the lights of Harbor Town. Captain Jack said we had better move to calmer water and anchor again. We had used all the fresh water on board and had no soft drinks left. I asked Dickie if he wanted to anchor again or go back to Harbor Town. He said go to Harbor Town. It was only about two miles and it turned out we would have to go back there anyway to get the right channel. On the way there, all of our 12-volt system went out. We tied up at the fuel dock in Harbor Town at 12:10 a.m. Just about the time we were tying up, the wind started blowing a gale and it started raining.

# Fresh Tales from a Native Gunner

The next morning we got up and everything was dead. Neither engine would start. I went over and woke up Bob and Evelyn Busk. They are friends of mine who have retired and live on their fifty-six-foot Chris Craft Roamer. They spent several summers tied up at the Coinjock Marina, and that is where I got to know them. They were surprised to see me. I told them of our plight, and they told me there was a Mr. Gresham who was about the only man you could get. They suggested we go to Isle of Hope Marina if we could get started.

When I got back to the boat somebody had talked to the dockmaster, and she had called Mr. Gresham. It was going to be a while before he could get there. We took this time to do a little grocery shopping and walked around Harbor Town. Mr. Gresham finally got there and said the starter on the starboard engine was melted and had shorted out a lot of other wires. We found after checking that the starter button on the starboard engine was stuck halfway in. That is probably what caused the problem, but can't be blamed on Captain Jack because it was dark when he started the engines in the inlet.

Mr. Gresham finally got the port engine started, and presented a bill of $60. We got underway at 11:30 a.m. on the February 17. It is only thirty-three miles from Hilton Head to Isle of Hope, Georgia. Just before you get to Thunderbolt, Georgia, the Intracoastal turns right, which Dickie told Captain Jack, but the Captain kept straight for about a mile until he finally admitted he was wrong and turned around.

We got to Isle of Hope Marina about 2 p.m., and they said they thought they could get us a starter. While they were working on the boat, we borrowed the marina van and went to the grocery and liquor store. We asked at the liquor store where we could get some oysters. They sent us to a place in Thunderbolt about seven miles away. We went there, got the oysters, put them in the van, then we decided we'd look at them. They were in clusters about ten inches in diameter, and the oysters were no wider than your little finger. We didn't want them, so we sent Robert to take them back and get our money back.

We went back to the dock and the dockmaster told us the man in the sailboat tied right across the dock from us was General Patten, the retired son of General George. He and some of his friends were getting ready to go on a cruise to the Caribbean. We did some laundry here, and Robert cooked hamburgers for supper.

The boys and Joe got a cab and went in to Savannah, about ten miles away. The rest of us turned in. I woke up when I heard Joe fall in the boat sometime before day. I'll say no more about that.

It was 11:00 a.m. before we got underway the next day. It cost over $700, and we still didn't have the gauges on the starboard engine fixed. The mechanic said our best chance was to get it fixed in Fort Lauderdale.

The weather was cool and misty. The trip through is nothing but mile after mile of marsh. We fueled at St. Simmons Island at 4:30 p.m. After we left there, we saw many beautiful homes on Jekyll Island.

We anchored that night in a deep creek just off the waterway approximately ten miles north of the Florida line. Captain Jack cooked cabbage and boiled potatoes and dumplings. He seasoned this with a piece of shoulder meat he cured himself. Let me say one thing—Captain Jack's navigating may leave something to be desired, but his cooking is first class.

On February 19, we got underway at 6:30 a.m. We saw lights in the distance, which Captain Jack said was a pulp mill. He said he could smell it. It turned out to be two government ships tied to a pier.

The *Deb Nan* at the Florida welcome station in Fernandina Beach, Florida. *Author's collection.*

# Fresh Tales from a Native Gunner

We passed the Florida welcome station in Fernandina Beach at approximately 7:30 a.m. From here on the trip was real nice. The weather was good, and we were in our shirt sleeves. We stopped in Jacksonville Beach and took on fuel, then proceeded on south past St. Augustine, Marineland and Daytona. We tied up in New Smyrna Beach at about 6 p.m. We took a shower and then got a cab to Blackbeard's Restaurant. This was recommended by the dockmaster and turned out to be good. They also had a raw bar so we had a few rounds of oysters, which were fresh but good. The steak was excellent. We came back to the boat, and all but the boys turned in. They went out on the town.

The next morning, Jack started the engines at 5:35 a.m. We were still in bed, but Bobby went out in his pajamas to help him cast off at 5:45 a.m. At 5:49, I felt the boat run solid aground. It was pitch dark outside. We finally got off after much grinding. There were times when I thought everything under the bottom of the boat was coming off. One time she laid right down on her side.

After we got off, one engine could only be idled and the other not run too fast, as it was vibrating so badly. We limped along through the north part of the Indian River to Titusville. We saw many big bunches of blackheads here. I called ahead on the VHF radio to Westland Marine to ask if we could get hauled out. The dockmaster said it would be Monday. (This was Saturday morning.) He said he could get a diver if that would help. We said get him there. The diver checked the damage and said the starboard prop had one blade folded up and the other one bent just a little. Dickie thought he had two spare props, but it turned out he only had one, but we were in luck because it was the one we needed. This was about 10:00 a.m. Bobby and Captain Jack had to catch a plane at 7:30 in Fort Lauderdale. They had to testify in a land case in Federal Court on Tuesday. Now, there is plenty of time between Saturday and Tuesday to fly back, but Bobby just had to make that plane. The rest of us figured Bobby had something hot on the docket for Saturday night or Sunday.

Bobby found out he couldn't rent a car there, but a Greyhound bus came through at 10:30 a.m. Bobby decided that he and Jack better catch it. After they left, I was promoted to acting Captain and Dickie to Navigator. I might add that we had no further problems from here to Fort Lauderdale with navigation or handling the boat.

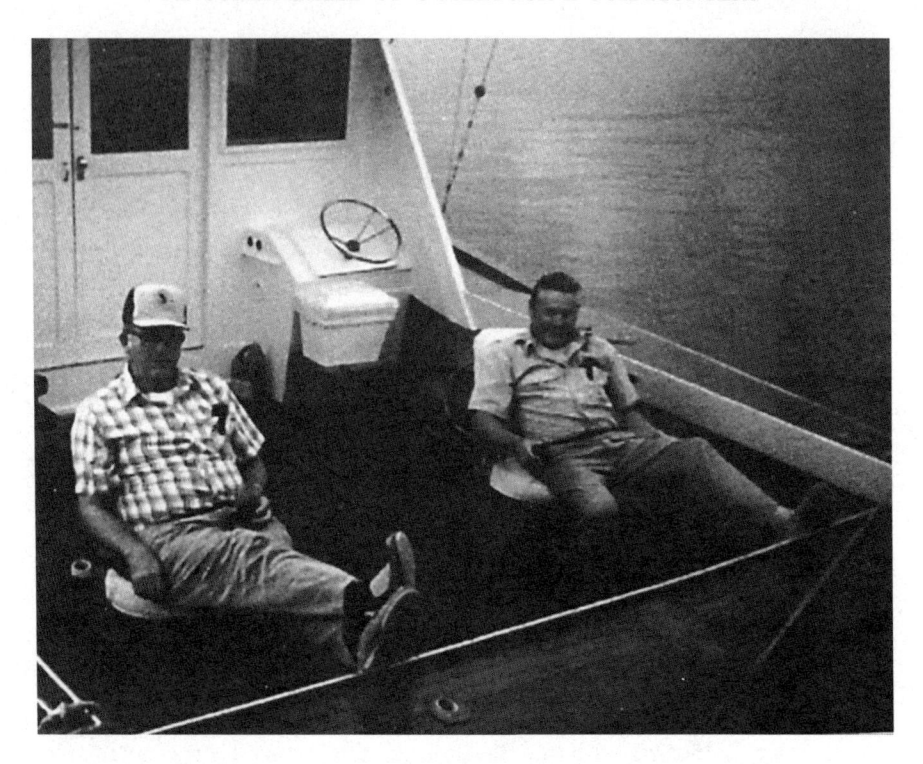

Travis Morris and Dickie Ferrell sitting back, enjoying the scenery. *Author's collection.*

We got underway from Titusville at 11:00 a.m. The weather was good (high 70s), and we were in short sleeves. After I got the boat back in the waterway, the boys ran it to Fort Pierce. Dickie kept checking the charts. We got to Ft. Pierce Municipal Marina at 5:30 p.m. There was a strong current here, and I docked the boat. After we fueled, we got tied up for the night. There was a large motor yacht tied up right behind us with some people on it, and right opposite us on the other side of the dock was a sword fishing boat. Dickie bought a dolphin from the boys on that boat, and they cleaned it for us. Robert was bringing it back on the boat when his foot slipped. He fell in the boat and dropped half of the fish overboard. Robert cooked the fish that night. That was the best fish I've ever eaten.

After supper, the boys went over and talked to the boys on the sword fishing boat. In the middle of the night, we heard a big noise on the forward deck that woke us all up. We thought someone was trying to steal the life raft. Dickie, Joe and I jumped up and ran out on deck only to find that it was a pelican. While we were up, we saw where the boys had changed clothes and gone out.

We left Ft. Pierce on February 21, at 7:20 a.m. When we got in front of Frances Langford's Outrigger Restaurant, I told Dickie I smelled hot rubber. He and Joe ran down to the engine room and found a water hose blown off the starboard engine. The gauges still didn't work on that engine, so we were lucky to catch it before any damage was done. It didn't take long to fix this and get on our way.

After you pass Stuart, twelve miles south, you soon enter Hobe Sound. I quote from *Palm Beach Life Magazine*, "Hobe Sound is the snootiest area in the United States." Jupiter Island is on the ocean side of Hobe Sound. The article goes on: "The wealth on Jupiter Island is the oldest and most independent in America." Some of the names are Hornblower, Harriman, Dillon, Mellon, Reed, Roosevelt, Adams, Scranton, Olin, Searle, Lamont, Duke, Doubleday, Cole, Pierrepont, Payson, Ford, Field and Weyerhauser. "Not the jet set like their neighbors in Palm Beach, they are the American cream. The aggregate wealth of the winter residents could thrice buy Saudi Arabia." Needless to say, there are some beautiful homes there that we could see from the waterway. We could not take pictures of them because we were not close enough and they were back in the trees, but we could see them well with the binoculars.

We got to Spencer's Marina in Palm Beach at 1:20 p.m. We fueled up. The dockmaster wanted to know who put the top on the flying bridge. I told him "Dagwood" from Aydlett, North Carolina. Dagwood was the best person I've ever known to design and build canvas tops for yachts. He put them on new Hatteras Yachts at the factory in New Bern, North Carolina.

*Billy Ferrell, Robert Ferrell and Dickie Ferrell. Author's collection.*

After fueling, we took showers and did the laundry. The rest of the day, we just relaxed.

As soon as we got there, Joe was looking for the phone number of a girl he knew there twenty-five years ago. He found her number, but couldn't get an answer. As soon as we washed clothes and got a shower Joe went ashore. About 2:00 or 3:00 a.m., we heard him blundering in. He got up with the girl, but she wouldn't let him come over. We assumed she had someone living with her, or she was married. We asked him if he thought she would be sitting there waiting for him after twenty-five years! He kept mumbling about two Doberman Pincers she had. We never did find out if he actually went there, but he did say he didn't see her. Before he finally hushed and went to sleep, he kept talking about how much he loved Holly. He bumped his head on the top of the boat, and then quietly settled in, except for the snoring.

We left Palm Beach about 7:40 a.m. but had to wait for several bridges and had a slow, uneventful, scenic trip to Fort Lauderdale. As soon as you get out of Lake Worth, it is a canal all the way to Fort Lauderdale. Each side of the canal is lined with either private homes or condominiums.

Bobby Ferrell and Joe Ferrell Jr. on the Intracoastal Waterway between Palm Beach and Fort Lauderdale, Florida. *Author's collection.*

# Fresh Tales from a Native Gunner

In Fort Lauderdale, we turned right in front of the Bahia Mar and went up the New River to Broward Marine. I have never seen as many big boats concentrated in one place in my life as there were on the New River. This is a narrow, winding river with hardly room for two boats to meet when you consider that there are boats tied up on each side of the river. There are also some nice houses there. The Armour meat people have a place here, as does Author Godfrey.

Broward Marine is a boatyard and not a marina. They don't have showers or laundry. It is an excellent boatyard where they build boats eighty feet and up. They put us under a shed. This was about 4 p.m. They said they would work on the boat the next day.

We got a taxi up to a steak house on the Seventeenth Street Causeway. The meal was good and reasonable. About the time we were finished, an old Swede who was about half drunk came by and wanted to talk. At first, he thought I was the daddy of all that crew! I know I look old, but not that old!

On February 23, we worked. The boys refinished the teak while Joe, Dickie and I cleaned the boat and polished the bright work. That afternoon, Robert put new belts on the starboard engine, which was no easy job. The electrician got our electrical problem fixed.

Late that afternoon, Mr. Etheridge, Robert's grandfather, came over and carried the boys home with him. Joe didn't feel too good, so he stayed aboard that night. Dickie and I went to a seafood house for supper and then to the revolving bar at the top of Pier 66. About 11:00 p.m., we came down, and Captain Jack and Bobby were waiting for us in the lobby. They had that propeller with them they had brought from Hatteras.

The next day was another morning of work. Jack took the water pump off the port engine and carried it up to the shop to be rebuilt.

With everything fixed except the compass, which was to be fixed at the Bahia Mar, we got underway at about 2:00 p.m. and headed for the Bahia Mar, with Dickie at the helm. We were afraid of what the bill would be at Broward, but it turned out to be the most reasonable place we went.

Dickie turned the helm over to Captain Jack to dock at the Bahia Mar fuel dock. When we finally got to the dock, the dockmaster wanted to know if we had an airplane pilot or a boat captain. After fueling, the dockmaster directed us to our berth, 141B.

We proceeded over there and the dockmaster was waiting to catch our lines. Captain Jack roared up, started to back into the slip sideways, hit a piling, finally got in the slip and immediately shut down the engines. The dockmaster nearly broke his back trying to stop the boat with the lines. He just stood up, rubbed his back and shook his head. Here we were in this nice, big sport fisherman with all the varnish shining and the dock was full of other boaters watching the performance of Captain Jack. I felt like hiding in the cabin, but I had to help the dockmaster secure the boat.

Being at the Bahia Mar instead of Broward is like being on the oceanfront at Virginia Beach compared to Sligo Creek. Girls were everywhere, and the boys were so anxious to get ashore they wouldn't even go to Patricia Murphy's restaurant with us "old mice." They said they would eat a baloney sandwich. We had a nice meal and walked out on the dock and looked at a yacht from London that was at least 150 feet long. We went back to the boat and turned in. About 1:30 a.m., I heard Billy come in. I got up and talked to him a few minutes. He said Robert had found a good-looking girl, and Billy didn't know when he'd be in. He got in about 5 a.m. I got up at 6:30 and got my gear together. I left the Pepto Bismol and Alka Seltzer for Joe.

After saying goodbye to everybody, I walked to the Bahia Mar Hotel and got a taxi to the airport. Thus ended a most enjoyable trip.

A trip down the Intracoastal Waterway has been one of my life's wishes since I was a little boy. I really appreciate Bobby and Dickie giving me a chance to go with them. We had a very congenial crew. It was great having Robert and Billy. They did a lot of work, and Robert is a good cook.

The rest were going on to the Bahamas and wanted me to go, but I had planned to go only as far as Fort Lauderdale and that took about the amount of money I felt like I could afford to spend on the trip. Bobby and Dickie said it wouldn't cost me another cent if I'd just go with them. I really appreciated the offer but I got to thinking Bimini is a little island out there in a big ocean. If Captain Jack was getting lost in Albemarle and Pamlico Sounds, I didn't think I wanted to take a chance on hitting that Island. There was no such thing as a GPS back then. The depth finder didn't work, and the Loran was outdated and didn't work. They were going to get the compass swung (compensated) in Fort Lauderdale.

I think I should say there is no malice behind the remarks I made about Jack Hoffler. I just told it like it happened, and I felt it made more amusing reading than if I had left it out.

Dickie asked me to call Mary Hadley Griffin from Palm Beach and inquire about Jack's abilities since he had carried her boat to the Islands. She assured me he was a competent captain, knew a lot of people in the Islands and had probably been there a hundred times. He takes good care of the boat and seems to be very conscientious. I'm sure his navigation was better in the ocean than in the Intracoastal, or they would have been on television where Castro had them.

## AND NOW FOR THE REST OF THE STORY, AS PAUL HARVEY SAYS

The following comes from a story in the June 6, 2004 edition of the *Daily Advance* by Bob Montgomery and from me talking to Jack Hoffler in his home. I went there one day after this article came out, to buy a duck boat from him. I brought this up and he gave me a copy of a documentary tape they made of him.

Now you have to remember when we made this trip to Florida in 1982, we didn't know any of the following. Jack didn't talk about it. The fortieth anniversary of D-Day was in 1984, and it became a big event. That day honored all the aging veterans that took part in the liberation of France from German occupation.

They, the people who made the documentary, found out that Jack was the youngest man in the Normandy Invasion. He was raised in Hertford, North Carolina. He was fourteen years old when he enlisted in the Navy in August 1943, at the Naval Recruiting Station in Elizabeth City. His father was dead, and all his brothers were in the service. He had to have parental consent saying he was seventeen years old. His mother wouldn't sign for him, so he got his brother-in-law to. He only weighed 107 pounds. He said he ate five pounds of bananas and drank over a gallon of water to put on enough weight to pass the physical. He was still underweight, but they took him.

The acknowledgement came in a letter years ago from former President Harry Truman, and again in 1994 from President Bill Clinton, who invited Hoffler to personally attend a D-Day ceremony in 1994 at Omaha Beach. I had another friend who was in the Normandy Invasion, Cyrus Aydlett, though he was older than Jack.

Jack has been interviewed as part of World War II commemorations by the History Channel, Fox News and is one of many featured in the colorful and comprehensive book *D-Day: The Greatest Invasion—A People's History* by Dan Vander Vat.

Jack said he was a gunner on a Landing Craft, Vehicle, Personnel (LCVP). He said they were running boats with supplies and ammunition to the front line soldiers and bringing back the wounded, all while bullets and explosions blurred his vision and hearing. On the night of the June 7, his boat hit an underwater mine and sank. He remembers jumping overboard and swimming to the beach about fifty yards away, laying with the dead, the wounded and the survivors all night.

When he returned to the beach, he was assigned the task of a "straggler," piling up the dead bodies from combat. "We prayed for darkness every day," he said. "It was hell."

He said the biggest obstacle the first couple of days was the never-ending artillery fire from German "big guns" that were in fortified bunkers on the high ground. The guns were eventually silenced by the Allied advance inland.

"You could hear shells coming across the field like a storm," he said. "If you heard them crackling, you hit the dirt."

He also ventured inland to Cherbourg France, where he delivered ammunition, rations and medical supplies. On his way back with two other men on a Jeep, they came under bombardment. A shell exploded, and he was blown into a latrine and pinned under a truck for an hour, with pieces of shrapnel in his left wrist and left leg. When he awoke, he couldn't believe he was still alive.

He was taken to a hospital in England and then back to the United States to a naval hospital in Chelsea, Massachusetts. After he recovered, he returned to the naval hospital in Norfolk, Virginia. He was ready to be redeployed to the Pacific, but the captain of the PT boat to which he had been assigned sent him back to a hospital in Portsmouth, Virginia, where he received a medical discharge in August 1945.

Another person I knew from the area that was in the Normandy Invasion was Harold B. Johnson. He was from Elizabeth City. He was sixteen when he joined the Navy. He got his daddy to certify that he was seventeen. I knew Harold when I was in the trucking business. He was in the long-distance trucking business also.

# The *Wild Goose*

The name of the forty-eight foot Sportfisherman *Deb Nan*, as I told you in the story, was changed to *Wild Goose* because *Deb Nan* sounded like "dead man" on the VHF radio.

After the Florida trip, Bobby and Dickie kept the boat maybe a year and decided to sell it. This was a wood boat, and those were getting hard to sell because everything was going to fiberglass.

I managed to give the boat to a school in Fort Lauderdale. They got a good tax right off and a little money. Dickie, Herbert Lange (a good friend of mine and retired Master Chief Engineman in the Coast Guard) and I delivered the boat to the Bahia Mar in Fort Lauderdale.

On the way down, we tied up in Southport, North Carolina, one night. The next morning we got up and started out early. Soon one engine started running hot. We turned around and went back to the marina. Lange found out the freshwater pump was not circulating. The engines were Johnson & Tower engines, which are just souped up 671 Detroits. One thing about those old engines is you can find parts for them anywhere.

Lange knew the fish buyer in Southport, who was called "Cash Caroon." He was from Lowland, North Carolina, where Lange's wife, Iva, was from. Lange went and found Cash, and he let us have the water pump off an old 671 he had up there in the yard. Lange put that on and we were on our way.

Everything went fine until we got to Jacksonville Beach, Florida. We got up early Thanksgiving morning and left Beach Marine. We hadn't even gotten to the bridge when the engine started running hot again. We came back to the marina, and Lange took the pump off. We found out a shipyard was open on Thanksgiving Day. We got a taxi up there. They said they could fix it, but it would be awhile.

I well remember the workers all had a good Thanksgiving dinner brought in, and Dickie, Lange and I were eating nabs and Coca Colas. I never wanted turkey so bad in my life.

We got the pump fixed and came back to the boat. Lange put it on. Then we got a taxi to a grocery store and bought some salmon and I don't remember what else. We came back to the boat and Dickie cooked it and we had a good supper.

We didn't have any more trouble and delivered the boat to Fort Lauderdale.

# The *Frances M*

In 1985, our daughter, Ruth Morris Ambrose, was just getting over a bout with cancer. Ruth loves boats like I do. Frances and I decided to take Ruth and our friends Herbert and Iva Lange to Fort Lauderdale on our boat, which was an old forty-foot wood Owens that Herbert Lange and I kept in Palm Beach condition. I won't go into a lot of details because I just took you on a trip to Fort Lauderdale.

We stayed at the Bahia Mar in Fort Lauderdale for nine days. They treated us as if we had a 100-foot yacht. I rented a car, and we went up to Palm Beach one day and down to Miami to see Dodson Mathias another good friend that was from Currituck. He was senior vice-president of South East Bank. I took them to a lot of other places around south Florida.

Ruth and Frances flew back home. Lindy Dunn, a close friend of mine from Rocky Mount, flew down to Fort Lauderdale and came back with us as far as Morehead City, North Carolina. He got off there, and Wayne Taylor got on and went on to Coinjock with us, which was our home port. Dodson Mathias got on in Fort Lauderdale and came up as far as Jacksonville Beach with us.

It was always a dream of mine to make the trip to Florida on the Intracoastal Waterway, but I never thought I'd get the chance. Between my friends' boats and my boat, I've been lucky enough to have made the trip seven times. At the time of this trip, Lindy Dunn had a sailboat but had never been down the waterway to Florida. After this trip, he bought three

# Another Breed of Currituck Duck Hunters

The *Frances M* leaving Beach Marine in Jacksonville Beach, Florida, in October 1985. We had just put Dodson Mathias off to catch a plane back to Miami. Lindy Dunn had just thrown the lines off and was climbing back up on the bridge with Herbert Lange and myself for the trip north. *Author's collection.*

different motor yachts, on which he rode me many miles. He's flown me many miles on his plane as well.

I'm sorry to say my first wife, Frances, and Lindy have both gone on to meet their maker. Both died with cancer.

# About The Author

Travis Morris is a native of Currituck County, North Carolina. He was born in Coinjock, the only child of Edna Boswood and Chester Ralph Morris.

After high school, he served in the Coast Guard for three years before attending Campbell College for a year and a half. He did almost anything he could to make a living and stay in Currituck, including farming, owning a long-distance trucking business, guiding duck hunters and commercial fishing. He ran Monkey Island Club four years while in the process of selling it, and three miles of beach from sound to ocean for the Penn Family. He and John High started Piney Island Club in 1983. He is still a member.

In 1970, Travis and his wife, Frances Meiggs Morris, started Currituck Realty, Inc., which he still owns and operates. They had four children together: Walton Morris, Ruth Morris Ambrose, Wayne Morris Sawyer and Rhonda Lee Morris. Frances died in 1992, and Travis married Jo Ann Hayman in 1995. She has one child, Jackie Lee.

Visit us at
www.historypress.net